TABLE OF CONTENTS

INTRODUCTION

WHAT CAN WE HOPE TO ACHIEVE?

When we are working with dementing clients and their families, there are several areas of human need which can be filled through the planned use of music, and the precis which appears below is an outline of the contents of this handbook, each one being developed at greater length in the appropriate chapter.

Before we start to plan our programs for dementing persons and their relatives, we need to have a firm basis of theoretical knowledge of the nature of the dementias, so that we may know - if this is possible - how it feels to the sufferer himself as he develops a dementing condition, what it is like for any of us to observe a relative or friend gradually become demented, what it is like to care for dementing persons in an institution of any kind, and so on.

We need this knowledge in order to work as members of the clinical team, making the best use of our resources in music and in therapy, thereby bringing some measure of relief, comfort and (for those aspects of dementia which are amenable to change) a degree of improvement.

As those involved in palliative care have said (and music therapy in dementia is not dissimilar to music therapy for the dying), mere hand-holding, the exclusive attention to psychosocial needs, is too soft an option. We must be concerned with the whole person and his family, employing the utmost in technical expertise as well as offering empathy and compassion.

Chapter 1 provides an outline of current knowledge about various dementing processes. There will be, the author believes, a loss of foundation to the work with dementing clients unless one has a firm theoretical basis for decisions about the direction the work should take.

We can sum up the characteristics of the dementing process as involving memory loss to the extent that independent home life is no longer safe and, eventually, the simplest of self-care becomes impossible. There will be difficulties of communication both conceptually and verbally; often there will be anger and paranoid ideation, intrusive behaviour and general frailty.

But what do we see, what do we think and what do we feel when we see a person with these problems?

- Fear....................."Perhaps that is how I will end up one day!"
- Pity.....................wanting to make up for the losses the person has experienced?
- Revulsion.............at stained and chaotic clothing, perhaps with an odour if there has been a recent episode of incontinence?
- Bewilderment.........at seeing meaningless grimaces, hearing mumbling, or baseless anger and shouted accusations?
- Anger...................that human life can come to this state?
- Helplessness..........that there is little we can do to effect change?
- Love and caring......a longing to give care and affection to the unloved?

We may think and feel all these - they are not mutually exclusive and, from time to time, are shared by professional and family alike, and it is not surprising that some people's first response is to "want out", or to distance themselves from dementing and incontinent persons by referring to them as "the Babies".

The music therapist is fortunate in that even a person with advanced dementia will probably respond a little to music, and this helps us to deal with the feelings of helplessness to which we are all prey at one time or another.

This book looks at how the dementias affect our clients, it looks at the way the dementing process affects observers and carers, and it looks in detail at how music in therapy brings some sense of individuality, an experience of caring and creativity, fun and stimulation. Most of all, although the dementing process is necessarily progressive, it looks at hope!

In what areas of need can we expect to help by using music as a therapeutic medium?

We can expect to build bridges between the isolated and lonely, and, even if such bridge-building is only a temporary measure, it is still worthwhile. We can hope to reduce aggression and wandering, we can help to give a sense of reality to the environment together with affirmation of the worthwhile nature of the individual.

We can offer some measure of choice even for those who are in an advanced stage of dementia, and this too enhances the sense of individuality - often denied to the dementing person in an institution.

We can hope to deal with some of the many and varied griefs and losses which flow from a dementing process, for both the individual and, more particularly, for the family.

We can hope to provide a means of enjoyment and personal satisfaction, to counteract at least some of the sadness, and to maintain some sense of creativity and **fun**, which is usually lacking in institutional life! There is, of course, a difference between recreational music and music therapy and this will be discussed in Chapter 8, but enjoyment and an increase in happiness is part of both recreation and therapy for those whose life otherwise tends to be drab and uneventful.

We can hope to achieve some useful changes in behaviour, although they are probably short-lived. But even if changes to a more normal mode of behaviour are only temporary in nature, they do help staff who are in daily contact with dementing people to see more potential in them.

We can hope to achieve maintenance mobilisation, and - for people with a condition which makes formal physiotherapy necessary - we can help in the interpretation and performance of whatever movements and treatments are needed.

We may also help to stabilise problems with circadian rhythms, in which there is day/night reversal; this is aided by the provision of stimulating programmes through the day, of which music would be one. When the author visited the Meridian Centre outside Baltimore, Maryland, (U.S.A.), figures were given which showed that, with the implementation of a day-long programme of stimulation and activity, the need for night-time sedation had disappeared. The implications are probably that, if we keep people happily busy through the day, they will not nod off to sleep in daytime hours and are therefore likely to sleep normally at night.

We can help in the maintenance of the dementing person at home, giving support to both sufferer and carers.

There is as yet no firm theoretical rationale for the use of music in therapy for dementing clients; we are working on an empirical basis only at present. There are, however, probably several factors involved to explain the outcome of our work:

- We are using old, well-established memory traces.
- Music is a nonthreatening activity with (usually) pleasant associations from past experiences[1].
- One writer has demonstrated the strong metabolism of glucose in the nondominant hemisphere during time in which subjects were listening to music[2].
- Although there is no exact differentiation between the hemisphere for music and speech, there is a general localisation of control for music in the nondominant hemisphere[3], so that even when normal propositional speech is lost, the person can enjoy music and perhaps sing words/melody[4].
- In the aphasia of dementia it seems likely that we are not seeing the aphasia of the stroke victim so much as a general failure of communication caused by apraxia and agnosia, caused

---

[1]Bright R. "Music in geriatric care". *Musicgraphics*, New York, 1980, p 6

[2]Mazziotta J.C. "Tomographic mapping of human cerebral metabolism: auditory stimulation" *Neurology*, Sept. 1982, **32**, (9), pp 921-937

[3]Gates A. & Bradshaw J.L. "The role of the cerebral hemispheres in music". *Brain and language*, 1977, **4**, pp 403-431

[4]Bright R. *Practical planning in music therapy for the aged.* Alfred International, (Sherman Oaks, CA), 1984, p 18.

by parietal lobe dysfunction[5] plus cognitive loss. These are characteristic of Alzheimer-type dementia as contrasted with the occasional dementia of Parkinson's disease[6].

- Responses to music are almost universally noted in Down's syndrome, and this may be significant in view of possible genetic links between Alzheimer's disease and Down's syndrome[7].

Can we hope that music or any other stimulation will slow down the processes of organic dementia? Sometimes it would appear that this is possible because behaviour may change for the better, either during the session or for a time afterwards. People may function better cognitively with reduced wandering, reduced aggression, increased social interaction and attention to their surroundings.

But the author believes that we are not in fact changing the dementia so much as stimulating the resources that remain, and that we are also dealing with the depression, the unexpressed anger and bewilderment of the sufferer.

The fact that demented persons behave so much better after music therapy, so much more like their normal selves, may in fact be an indictment of the way they are "normally" treated!

To work with the demented client or group of clients and with their families too is a challenge, but one which brings its own satisfactions.

If we attempt to comprehend what it is like for our clients who have a dementing condition, if we try to understand what it must be like to live in a continual fog (as it was described by a man who improved dramatically after a shunt was implanted to reduce the dementia caused by normal-pressure hydrocephalus), if we can imagine what it is like to forget where the bathroom is, to cease to know when we need to empty the bladder or bowels, what it is like to be called "Dear" or "Pop" rather than our own names - if we can even begin to understand all this, then we shall have taken our first steps in therapy.

If we can assess people's needs and plan our programs to meet therapeutic needs - building up self-esteem, giving dementing persons an experience of achievement and success, helping them to communicate their feelings, hopes and fears, using our knowledge and our empathy to give comfort and reassurance - then we shall succeed beyond our dreams in using music to bring happiness and a sense of individuality to those whom the world tends to write off as valueless.

CONTRA-INDICATIONS

Despite out enthusiasm for music, we must not make the mistake of assuming that it is appropriate for everyone. There will be some for whom music has such tragic associations that it brings unmitigated distress, for which there is no solution, and such persons should be allowed to withdraw from music programmes.

Sensori-neural deafness which causes the phenomenon of recruitment is another reason why music is inappropriate for some older people. In recruitment (characteristic of Menière's disease) loud sounds cause acute physical pain.[8] Someone who is cognitively intact can usually explain what is happening, but a dementing person may show only anger, and is at risk of being labelled "Difficult" if we are unable to work out the reason for his distress. This same phenomenon also explains why some hearing-impaired people complain of not being able to hear what is said, but - when the speaker raises the voice only a little - say angrily, "There is no need to shout!"

We must be aware of the difficulties of our dementing clients and permit them the dignity of saying, "No thank you!"

---

[5]Chase T.N. et al "Parietal lobe involvement in Alzheimer's disease" *Lancet*, July 23, 1983, (ii), p 225

[6]Rabins P.V. "Psychopathology of Parkinson's disease" *Compr. psychiatry*, 1982, **23**, 5, pp 421-429

[7]Heston L. "Alzheimer's dementia and Down's syndrome: genetic evidence suggesting an association". *Annals of the New York academy of science*, 1982, **396**, pp 29-39

[8]Deweese D.D. & Saunders W.H. *Textbook of otolaryngology.* C.V. Mosby. 1960. pp 307-308

CHAPTER 1

THE NATURE AND PREVALENCE OF DEMENTIA: IMPLICATIONS FOR THE THERAPIST

What is "dementia"? In the past the word itself has frequently been used as a synonym for "insanity" - so that as long ago as the 16th Century, a "Dement" was an insane person (vide Oxford English Dictionary). Even today an exasperated parent may say to a child, "You'll drive me demented if you go on doing that!"

The reactions to the word as indicating insanity are also seen in some elderly sufferers who, in the earlier stages, experience a deep fear of "going insane," which is seen as somehow morally reprehensible. (Such people need reassurance even if cognitively it appears that they may not understand what is being said.)

In more recent times, the term dementia was often combined with "senile" so that "senile dementia", a loss of memory and normal behaviour, was seen as being a fairly normal part of human aging.

Although there are many causes of a dementia syndrome, the most common form of dementia is Alzheimer's disease or dementia of the Alzheimer type, and these terms have now been accepted into everyday speech and journalism.

At one time the term "Alzheimer's disease" was used only to describe an early-onset dementia, probably in middle-age, and later-onset disease was described as Senile Dementia. However, it is now recognised, as various writers have described[1], that the pathology for the two is identical, the same neurofibrillary plaques and tangles being found at post mortem. There are suggestions, however, that there may be a genetic influence in the development of early-onset dementia[2]. Early onset Alzheimer's is often named AD type 2 and late-onset as AD-1.[3]

It may be, as some workers have commented, that it is over-diagnosed, that many people labelled as having Alzheimer's have in fact some other form of dementia. However, it is probably a healthy mistake, in that it is better than the out-moded term "Senile dementia", since it avoids the associations of it being a normal part of human aging, with - at the same time - overtones of judgement.

The common use of the name Alzheimer's disease has made the emotional shock of dementia easier to bear for many people, both relatives and the sufferers themselves (in the early stages when they are aware that they are deteriorating). To have a named disease, even if the cause of it is unknown, is somehow easier to bear than merely being labelled "senile."

There are, however, occasional disadvantages both to sufferer and family in this blanket use of the term Alzheimer's disease to describe dementia.

One man aged sixty-three, who had suffered for many years from progressive supra-nuclear palsy, did - in the process of the advancing disease - develop some dementia and problems with wordfinding. But when placed in a day centre catering for persons suffering from Alzheimer-type dementia, he was deeply unhappy, because he felt that he did not fit in. Similarly, his wife, taking part in meetings of ADARDS, (this being the acronym for the [Australian] Alzheimer's Disease and Related Disorders Society) found little relevance in the experiences or coping strategies of others who were caring at home for relatives with Alzheimer-type dementia, because her husband's needs and problems were markedly different.

Over-ready labelling as "Alzheimer's disease" may also lead to failure of diagnosis of what is actually a reversible condition. And it is not unknown for a temporary confusional state, the result of an infection, to be mistaken at first for dementia.

Writers today vary in the precision of their use of the term "dementia," and this has been discussed

---

[1]Sulkava R. "Alzheimer's disease & senile dementia of the Alzheimer type: a comparative study", *Acta neurol. Scand.* 1982, **65**, pp 636-650

[2]Pearce J.M.S. *Dementia - a clinical approach.* Blackwell, Oxford, 1984. pp 5-6.

[3]McLean S. "Assessing dementia, Part II: clinical, functional, neuropsychological and social issues" *Australia and New Zealand journal of psychiatry,* 1987, **21**, pp 284-304

succinctly in *The Lancet* by Brown and Marsden[4]. They quote Benton and Sivan[5] as saying that "dementia is simply a non-specific diagnosis of behavioural incompetence referable to brain disease." Certainly many people involved in the care of dementing persons would see this as adequate, but is it enough?

The answer may depend upon our reason for needing a definition. If we are concerned solely with whether or not a person is fit to manage his own life or whether he needs fulltime care, then a functional definition and diagnosis may well be all that is required. The danger of this approach is that we may thereby fail to investigate adequately the causes for the condition, and therefore miss finding those dementing conditions which are reversible. If, on the other hand, we are involved in scientific investigation of dementing processes, then the simple definition will not be enough. The definition adopted by each music therapist will depend on his or her work in this field, whether it is functional music therapy to improve the quality of living, or whether one is also involved in basic research in dementia.

Brown and Marsden comment that the DSM III definition is far more stringent than the Benton & Sivan description given above, and they quote the list below which follows the DSM III criteria[6], as establishing a firm diagnosis of dementia.

- Loss of intellectual abilities of sufficient severity to interfere with social or occupational living
- Memory impairment
- At least one of the following:
    1. Impairment of abstract thinking
    2. Impaired judgement
    3. Other disturbances of higher cortical function
    4. Personality change
- State of consciousness not clouded
- Either evidence of a specific organic factor aetiologically relevant to the disturbance, or an organic factor can be presumed if conditions other than organic mental changes have been reasonably excluded and if the behavioural changes represent cognitive impairment in a variety of areas.

This discussion was part of a paper on the incidence of dementia in Parkinson's disease (This topic will be discussed later, see page 5.), but it gives an excellent background to any discussion of dementia, its manifestations and management.

The DSM III definition is not immutable (there have been, after all, earlier editions of this book of diagnostic criteria), and there has also recently been discussion as to the adequacy of these criteria for a diagnosis of dementia to be made[7]. The World Health Organisation book on orderly classification of disease and disabilities is also helpful[8]. Nevertheless, until such time as new criteria are accepted, the present DSM III listings provide us with a reliable starting point for the mid-1980's.

Dementia is often accepted as an irreversible sentence of inexorable deterioration, but we now know that many instances of dementia are in fact reversible. Gershon & Herman have discussed and summarised the need for clear differential diagnosis.[9]

---

[4] Brown R.G. & Marsden C.D. "How common is dementia in Parkinson's disease?", *Lancet*, December 1, 1984, pp 1262-1265.

[5] Benton A.L. & Sivan A.B.J. "Problems and conceptual issues in neuropsychological research in aging and dementia." *Jnl. clin. neuropsych.* 1984, pp 57-63.

[6] American Psychiatric Association. *Diagnostic and statistical manual of mental disorders.* 3rd Edition, Washington, DC, USA, 1980

[7] Jorm A.F. & Henderson A.S. "Possible improvements to the diagnostic criteria for dementia in DSM-III." *British journal of psychiatry,* 1985, **147**, pp 394-399.

[8] World Health Organisation "International classification of disease and disability." U.N.O., 1981.

[9] Gershon S. & Herman S.P. "The differential diagnosis of dementia." *Journal of American geriatric society.* Winter 1982, **30**, pp 58-66.

Some authorities, such as Pearce[10], give a figure of 10-15% of all conditions diagnosed as "Dementia" are reversible, treatable conditions.

He lists as conditions which - if treated appropriately, at the right time - may well be reversible:

- Trauma - resulting in, e.g., sub-dural haematoma, which can be surgically evacuated
- Anoxia - from hypoperfusion states
- Infections - from brain abscess, the sequelae of meningitis, encephalitis, fungal meningitis, neurosyphillis
- Deficiencies - of Vitamin B12, folic acid; pellagra, of thiamine (in Wernicke's encephalopathy, occurring in alcoholism; in the lifethreatening vomiting which sometimes occurs in pregnancy, and in other conditions which cause gross dietary insufficiency of Vitamin B1)
- Neoplasms - space-occupying lesions within the skull cause dementia by the pressure they exert upon the cortex
- Intoxications - e.g., barbiturates, bromides, alcohol, amphetamines, hallucinogens, organic poisons, solvents (as in the dementia caused by glue sniffing)
- Metabolic - hypo-thyroid, hypercalcaemia, pituitary dysfunction, Cushing's disease, hepatic encephalopathy, renal failure, dialysis dementia - caused by the presence of aluminium in the water used for dialysis
- Dynamic - such as obstructive or communicating ("normal pressure") hydrocephalus
- Vascular - multiple brain infarcts from emboli, thrombosis lacunal infarcts (characterised by the presence of "holes" in the brain tissue) and so on

Cummings[11] also lists conditions which cause dementia but which are reversible if treated adequately, for example: anticholinergic drugs such as those used in the treatment of Parkinson's disease, antihypertensive agents, anticonvulsant agents, digitalis, and many of the metals such as lead, manganese, gold and various others.

Varney has described a reversible steroid dementia[12] in subjects ranging in age from twenty-five to sixty-five.

Cummings quotes Learoyd[13] whose findings showed that 16% of all admissions to psychiatric hospitals in persons over sixty-five years of age were directly caused by psychoactive drugs.

Gurland provides a salutary list of the risks of failing to diagnose depression in the elderly[14]; we may cause unnecessary suffering, set up avoidable chronicity, promote suicide, premature retirement, poly-pharmacy, overuse of community and health facilities and services, unnecessary institutional admission, and so on. He also draws to our attention the incidence of "Ageism", where conditions which would lead to full-scale investigations in the younger person are accepted as inevitable in the elderly[15]. Ageism affects the consumer as well as the professional: a man in his 70's had accepted as the unavoidable consequence of aging a paralysis and weakness caused by cord compression from bony growth in the vertebrae which, if he had been younger, would have led him to seek investigation rather than - as actually occurred - the condition

---

[10]Pearce J.M.S. Op Cit. page 50 ff.

[11]Cummings J.L. "Treatable dementias" pp 165-183 in *The dementias*, ed. Mayeux & Rosen, no. 38 in the series, *Advances in neurology*, Raven Press, New York, 1983.

[12]Varney N.R. "Reversible steroid dementia." *American journal of psychiatry*, 1984, **141** (3), pp 369-372.

[13]Learoyd B. "Admissions to a psychiatric hospital" *Med. jnl. Aust.*, 1972, **1**, pp 1131-1133.

[14]Gurland B. & Tower J. *Differentiating dementia from non-dementing conditions in the dementias*, p 15.

[15]Gurland B. & Tower J. op cit, p 7

being discovered by accident when he sought help for a prostate problem!

Garcia[16] has written of the dangers of over-diagnosis of dementia, and Gurland[17], from Columbia's Center on Aging, has warned of the need to look for (and treat) depression in the apparently demented elderly; otherwise one may miss a diagnosis of pseudodementia. As he points out, many psychiatric illnesses, including severe depression, can cause pseudodementia because they lead to a failure of self-care, delusions of persecution, aggression and so on.

There is some controversy regarding the commonality between depression and dementia, and the existence of the syndrome of pseudodementia. Many workers, e.g., McAlister[18], believe that there is a disease entity of pseudodementia, in which a major depressive illness causes such failure of ordinary functioning as to mimic the appearance of an organic dementia, but which, by appropriate treatment measures (both pharmacological and by counselling, etc.), can be reversed. (Because of the extent of depression in dementia, the topic is mentioned throughout this book.)

McAlister has also written of the value of biochemical investigation in separating depression from dementia, discussing the dexamethazone suppression test[19]. A different position is that of Rabins and others[20] who believe that a depressive illness unmasks an underlying organic dementia, but that the depression causes the dementia to have greater effect on functioning than would otherwise occur. Thus the effective treatment of the depression appears to "cure" the dementia, but in fact the organic condition remains, below the surface, until such time as its further progress renders it unmistakable.

Many writers have discussed the phenomenon of pseudodementia. One of the most recent articles[21] is that of Bulbena and Berrios, working to analyse a sample population in Cambridge, U.K., who concluded that pseudodementia does appear to represent a separate disease entity correlated with delusions, unipolar disease, previous affective disorder with positive outcome, but negatively correlated with nonaffective diseases and confusion. They conclude that a diagnosis of pseudodementia is no guarantee of sustained recovery in the elderly, there being a high risk of relapse and/or of developing sequelae of various kinds.

From time to time one also hears discussion as to the existence of benign memory failure, in which memory is defective but there is none of the change of personality or other social losses described in the strict criteria for a diagnosis of dementia. There are those who reject the entity of benign memory failure, believing that it is necessarily a precursor to major dementia, even though the full picture may be delayed for some years. Others, such as Gurland et al, report their findings that there can be a benign memory dysfunction without a co-existing dementia[22].

We are often faced with a confusing picture in which we cannot be certain what is taking place. **The sudden onset of memory loss or behaviour changes should alert us to a reversible situation. But this is not always clearly understood by the onlooker, so that the diagnosis of irreversible dementia may stand until wiser council prevails, appropriate investigations are carried out and the underlying cause is dealt with.**

We see dementia in some cases of brain neoplasms, when the pressure of the tumour upon surrounding structures causes irrational and apparently demented behaviour. In a young subject, such behaviour would lead to high-technology investigations, but, sadly, older people are often misdiagnosed as dementing without proper investigations being carried out, and they may be wrongly assigned to nursing homes as a result. One such person, labelled as "hopelessly demented - nursing home placement only", was fortunate in that the area geriatrician refused to accept this label without investigation, and it was found that the woman had a space-occupying lesion. This was surgically removed and found to be benign, the patient made an

---

[16]Garcia B. et al "The overdiagnosis of dementia" *Journal of the American geriatric society*, 1981, **29**, pp 407 - 410.

[17]Gurland B. & Tower J. op cit, p 1 ff.

[18]McAlister T.W. "Pseudodementia, an overview" *American journal of psychiatry*, 1983, 140:5, pp 528 - 533.

[19]McAlister T.W. "Problems of distinguishing between Alzheimer-type dementia and depression." *American journal of psychiatry*, April 1982, **139**, pp 479-481.

[20]Rabins P.V. et al. "Criteria for diagnosing reversible dementia caused by depression. Validation by a two-year follow-up." *British journal of psychiatry*, 1984, **144**, pp 488-492.

[21]Bulbena A. & Berrios G.E. "Pseudodementia: facts and figures" *British journal of psychiatry*, 1986, **148**, pp 87-94.

[22]Pearce J.M.S op cit. p 3

uneventful recovery, went on a world tour, took a post as a housekeeper and continued to enjoy life for many years[23].

We need to be aware of the many diseases in which dementing processes are likely to be observed; these include multiple sclerosis,[24] the progressive supranuclear palsy mentioned above[25] (often confused with Parkinson's disease), Parkinson's disease itself - although, as Browne and Marsden pointed out in 1984, the prevalence is in fact far lower than has been stated.[26]

Parkinson's disease is a condition in which, amongst other problems, the facial expression is rendered inexpressive and apparently uninterested, similarly the vocal quality; there is a forward-leaning posture, the walking is severely impeded - at first slow, with failure to swing the arm(s). There is a difficulty in initiating movements and the gait shows extremely small steps, combined with a paradoxical speed, so that, once started, the sufferer may appear to hurry along.

The resting tremor too affects the hands and often the face and jaw also. ["Resting" is somewhat of a misnomer in describing the involuntary movements, in that deep sleep extinguishes the tremor, but it is so-called to distinguish it from the intention tremor of multiple sclerosis and other cerebellar dysfunctions, where the tremor only really starts as one tries to do something.]

The reason these physical signs are discussed at length is that the person with advanced Parkinson's disease may **look** demented when in fact he or she is inwardly alert, interested in what is going on, longing for lively conversation and human interest. But because of the flat, uninterested appearance, he may be written off as demented when this is far from the truth, even though there is a known incidence of true dementia in the disease. One Parkinson's patient gave her changed appearance as a major reason for her despair and suicide attempt.

Huntington's disease or any disease which involves involuntary choreiform movements may similarly "put people off" and reduce social contact. In Huntington's, there are jerky, purposeless movements which may be very strong, the gait is highly abnormal with strange darting movements of head and trunk, and although, in fact, the intellect may be relatively intact (memory may be impaired at varying stages in this degenerative disease, but intellect is likely to remain spared for much of the progress of the disease), the general appearance is of a "demented" person, who is thereby deprived of ordinary social contacts and relationships, and yet who desperately needs care and attention. Dementia in Huntington's[27] appears to be somewhat variable in incidence, so that it is often present, but we must nevertheless not assume that a person who is known to have the disease, whose facial expressions consist of contorted grimaces and whose body movements are wildly inappropriate, is incapable of enjoying normal group activities in music or in anything else which is relevant to his or her past experience or desire for future creativity.

In stroke, aphasia may also mimic dementia. When normal speech is obliterated and all that emerges when the sufferer tries to speak is meaningless jargon, when he is unable to understand or respond to anything which is said to him (as occurs in a global aphasia involving both input and output of word processing), it is easy to assume that the person is clinically dementing.

Persons with global speech deficits who also have concentration problems and perhaps also spatial losses (so that there is an inability to perceive part of one's surroundings), give a picture of major loss which causes extreme feelings of helplessness in the therapist, and this picture of inability to deal with life may indeed justify a label of functional dementing syndrome. (By "functional" is meant not the psychiatric term meaning that the person, subconsciously, mimics a disease which in fact he does not have, as with functional mutism or functional paralysis, but rather that the condition affects the person's life as if he indeed had the full blown clinical disease.) In practical terms, looking at the capacity of the person to run his own life independently, he or she may well be as impaired as if he had text book dementia, and it is probable that the person will have to be in institutional care unless relatives are especially committed to

---

[23]Geeves R.B. "Personal communication" (Hornsby-Kuringai Area Health Services, N.S.W., Australia)

[24]Tourtelotte W.W. et al "The use of P300 & dementia rating scale in the evaluation of cognitive dysfunction in multiple sclerosis." *Acta neurol. Scand.* 1984, **101**, pp 32-34.

[25]Benson D.F. "Sub-cortical dementia" in *The dementias*, Raven Press op cit., p 186.

[26]Brown & Marsden "How common is dementia in Parkinson's disease?", *Lancet*, December 1, 1984, pp 1262 - 1265.

[27]Caine E.R. et al. "Huntington's dementia" *Archives of General Psychiatry.* 1978, **35**, pp 377-386

home care and are free to concentrate their energies on the task.

We must recognise, however, the that sufferer from such global deficits may (because of the overall representation in the cortex of music skills) be able to enjoy music and may benefit from some reassurance even if only by the tone of voice and touch, so that the globally-aphasic client offers us an enormous challenge in care and therapy, and much of our work will resemble programmes devised for dementing persons, whether or not a firm diagnosis of dementia has been established.

There is controversy as to whether the effects of advanced alcohol-related brain damage constitute dementia, but if one examines the DSM III criteria together with the indications of advanced alcoholism, (even after detoxification we note, for example, inability to care for oneself, inability to plan and make decisions, loss of abstract thinking, changes of personality, impaired judgement, but without alteration of consciousness once detoxification has been achieved), it would appear that there are sufficient parallels to justify the serious consideration of dementia as being associated with advanced alcohol-related brain damage. However, it must be acknowledged that the preservation of islands of intact functioning, and the fact that to cease the intake of alcohol prevents further deterioration (so that the dementia is not an inexorable process of deterioration), lead some people to question whether dementia is, in fact, linked with alcohol-related brain damage.

In terms of needing to lead a protected and organised existence, in which someone takes responsibility for planning and provision of life support services of the simplest kind, the helplessness of the person with advanced alcohol related brain damage may well cause him to be seen as demented, even if he does not fit the strict criteria.[28]

The dementia of multi-infarct disease, in which the sufferer has had a series of small strokes, each resulting in a further deterioration of function, is also different from Alzheimer's, in that there are often islands of intact functioning rather than a global deterioration affecting every aspect of life. The tragedy of this condition is that the patient, because of the patchy nature of the areas of cortex which are affected in the earlier stages, may be to some extent aware of his own disintegration, and the consequent unhappiness has been observed showing itself as anger, suicidal despair, or generally difficult behaviour.

If we are not aware of the conditions in which dementia may occur, the stress it may bring to the carer, and aware too of the limiting effects which it has on the functioning of the individual patient, we may cause the person unhappiness and frustration because we have unreal expectations of what they "should" be able to do, in activities in music therapy, in any other activity or in everyday relationships.

As therapists we do not so much need to be able to recite the DSM III criteria as to know in practical terms how dementia affects our clients and the way we plan our work with them, our expectations of their functioning and how to set realistic goals, aims and objectives in our work.

We have to allow for memory failure, and treat each session as if it were the first, introducing ourselves to our clients as if for the first time, rather than expecting them to remember who we are and why we are there. Eventually it may occur that some individuals will remember who we are and what the purpose of our visit is. But we must not assume that this recognition has occurred until we know for certain.

We need to be aware that dementia leads to difficulty or total inability to communicate and understand ideas, and to process words in the brain (not merely a difficulty in pronunciation as such, which is termed dysarthria), and we must take these difficulties into account when planning programmes.

We must know that dementia frequently affects the body image of the sufferer, so that there are likely to be difficulties in copying actions or movements, and of carrying out purposeful movements on request (even to the extent that self-feeding becomes impossible), and this influences not only general mobility but also any programmes we may prepare for maintenance physical therapy. We may see, for example, that a person who is asked to stamp his feet may cross his legs, or if asked to smile may stick out his tongue. This is disconcerting to the uninformed!

---

[28]Edwards G. & Grant M. *Alcoholism: new knowledge and new concepts.* Croom Helm, London, 1977 p 195.

We shall need to have some measure of understanding (as far as this is possible for an observer to achieve), of the stresses of those who are full time carers of persons with advanced dementia, in the home or in hospitals/nursing homes, so that we may integrate the carers - if they wish it - in our programmes.

To sum up, it may be said that all who work with dementing persons, at any stage of the condition, need to have a broad general picture of the pathology, as well as the social and emotional effects upon the sufferer and his family. Only with such a background of knowledge can we bring the best possible help to our clients.

Note: Throughout this book there are references to Reisberg's descriptions of the stages in the dementing process, and it seems appropriate to give a summary of them here [29].

1. Normal phase	No cognitive decline.
2. Forgetfulness	Subjective complaints of memory loss only.
3. Early confusional	May get lost in familiar places, job decline. losing valuable objects, word-finding deficit, poor reading retention, denial + anxiety.
4. Late confusional	Decreased awareness of recent events and ability to travel, unable to perform complex tasks, denial predominates and defensive withdrawal from challenge occurs.
5. Early dementia	Unable to survive without assistance, unable to recall recent personal events, some temporal disorientation and dressing difficulties.
6. Middle dementia	Sometimes forgets spouse's name, unaware of recent events, disorientated for time & place, needs assistance with daily living activities. Personality and emotional changes include delusional behaviour, agitation, obsessive symptoms.
7. Late dementia	All verbal abilities lost. Assistance needed for toileting and feeding, lose basic psychomotor skills, frequently neurological signs and symptoms are present

[29] Reisberg B. et al "An ordinal functional assessment tool for Alzheimer's-type dementia." *Hosp. Community psychiatry,* 1985, **36**, pp 593-595

CHAPTER 2

ASSESSMENT OF THE DEMENTING CLIENT

There are several questions we need to ask ourselves when planning to assess patients who appear to be suffering from dementing processes:

1. Are we to be involved in major history-taking in order to reach a diagnosis or are our decisions and opinions likely to be only a small part of the total input of the team?

The depth of our assessment will depend on the answer to this, and the answers to the next question.

2. Why are we doing an assessment anyway?

- Because we need to contribute something to the diagnosis and decision-making process?
- Because we want to do research on dementia ?
- Because we want to see whether our treatment approach is suitable for the patient?
- Because we hope to demonstrate quantitatively that patients are "better" after our treatment than they were before?
- Because we want to find out what approach is most likely to lead to improved quality of life for the patient?
- Because we hope to diminish grief and guilt in the family?

Upon the answers to these questions will depend the design of our assessment protocol.

- If we are to be involved in the major decisions as to whether or not a patient has an organic dementia and not a major depressive illness, then we shall be involved in history-taking from the family and - although less likely - from the patient himself. It may not be necessary to take a full history if we are employed as therapists, but all of us need to use our utmost in powers of observation of how the patient behaves. Do we know of any factors which may affect behaviour, as, for example, when a recent change of environment throws an elderly person into a state of temporary confusion, which may mimic dementia but is not an organic state? A bereavement, the moving of a supportive relative to another town, anxiety about a spouse - for an elderly and frail person such matters can cause the onset of an agitated depression which closely mimics dementia.

- We want to do research?
  Fine, because all of our urges to find things out - why, how, when - are only research without the formal title, and without this need to find out, no new knowledge would be learned. But we must remember that research can be very seductive, and can be done from various motives as well as the betterment of our clients - the search for professional fame and personal aggrandisement, money (because a higher degree probably leads to better pay!) and so on.

  There is nothing wrong with career advancement, so long as it does not become THE driving force behind our work. The risks of this are obvious!

  We must also remember that if we are involved in research on, say, the preservation of music skills in early dementia, we are likely to want to investigate to the utmost in order to know which skills have been retained and which have been lost.

  We need to remind ourselves that such rigorous investigation may, by emphasising the losses, and the limits at which those losses become obvious, cause agitation and sadness to the client, who is reminded yet again that he is not what he used to be. The ethics of such investigations must be borne in mind. (See below for possible methods of "testing without trauma.")

- If we are trying to find out whether our treatment approach is suitable for any individual client, then we shall need to draw upon other people's results - those of cognitive status memory and concentration span as tested by the neuropsychologist, the orthoptist's report on visual field losses, as well as on visual acuity, the physician's report on stamina and any special risk factors such as compromised lung or cardiovascular function. And so on.

- If we wish to find out whether our patients are better after receiving our particular treatment approach than they were before, we shall need some rating scale, e.g., which reliably assesses depression and the absence of depression, since to rate changes in depression is a very helpful way of assessing the response to treatment, in that depression and unhappiness are probably the most disastrous consequences of dementia in everyday life. But other measurements are also useful, such as assessment of aggressive behaviour, and whether changes occur as a consequence of music therapy.

- If we are working in a multi disciplinary team approach, there is an additional challenge in assessment - it is difficult often to determine exactly how much of the improvement is due to our intervention in music therapy and how much to other factors.

- If our chief aim is to bring a greater degree of happiness, then our assessment will be largely a matter of careful observation in the course of an everyday conversation, our consultations with the family playing a major part in our decisions.

Although it is tempting to establish our own rating criteria when assessing the cognitive function of our patients, in preparation for planning programmes or as part of research to validate the reliability of our methods, there are so many disadvantages in inventing new systems that it is safe to say, "DON'T DO IT !"

By using rating scales which are already assessed for reliability, one's work has greater credibility than if one invents one's own systems and then has to go on to defend the reliability of the system. It is far more practical and cost effective to use an appropriate scale which has already had its reliability demonstrated, so that one can spend available time on the business in hand rather than, e.g., testing rater reliability, whether the assessment/questionnaire or whatever really does test what it sets out to test, and so on.

There are, of course, reliable methods such as the 10cm line for a visual analogue, for which the basic principle is long established, and one can use it for a particular purpose by carefully choosing appropriate terms to use at each end of the line, so that this method lends itself to a certain amount of innovation. But to fill out such a form demands a high level of abstract thinking, in order to transform one's feelings into a spatial mode of expression, and represent the extent of those feelings by a mark on a straight line. Such abstraction is unlikely to be possible for a person with any substantial dementia. (This analogue method can certainly be used for assessment of changes achieved, but the rating must be done by observers.)

But if one is entirely innovative, then all one can say at the end is, "This method seems to give a reliable means of assessing...." It may be that your method will appeal to others, who will go on to use it extensively so that a body of professional literature will grow up based upon your innovation. Throughout the history of statistical method there have always been innovators - otherwise the standard inventories and questionnaires which we are accustomed to use would not exist! But it is only occasionally that someone "designs a better mouse trap" and the world beats a path to his door! So, if there is a reliable and usable rating scale, already validated and ready for use, which is applicable to the matter which you wish to investigate, then use it, and save yourself an enormous hassle.

When considering inventories and assessment scales, it is important to recognise that different tests have different thresholds as to what constitutes a "case." If, for example, one wished to find all potential suicides in a given population, one would devise a system with a low threshold, since it is more important to pick up all potential suicides, even at the risk of picking up some who are actually NOT at risk, rather than having a high threshold and missing some who truly are at risk.

On the other hand, if one wishes to identify all persons who need full psychiatric assessment and admission, one would prefer to have a high threshold, with the possibility of missing out on some people who may be in need, rather than having a low threshold and thereby picking up, and labelling as "cases," some people who are NOT actually ill or in need of admission.

Similarly, when assessing the significance of one's results, one may assume that all the outcome is due to chance, thereby rejecting some results which were, in fact, due to the experimental techniques (a type 1 error) or, conversely, we may assume that all of the results are due to the technique and reject the possibility that chance played a part in the outcome (a type 2 error).

When considering assessment of dementia, there will certainly be many people whose results are equivocal, people who, for one reason or another, present worse at the time of assessment than they do in everyday living, because of anxiety, fear of unfamiliar surroundings, and so on.

In dementia, one of the most widely used scales is the Mini-mental state of Folstein[1]. This has been used over a long period of time, and has stood up to rigorous testing to ensure that it tests what it sets out to test, and that the assessment of scores as indicating the presence or absence of dementia is accurate. This assessment is not lengthy, and, over a number of years, has been found to give a reliable basis for a tentative diagnosis of dementia to be made, when taking into account also the multiplicity of psychosocial factors which influence the lives of elderly at-risk clients.

Another most useful descriptive scale is that of Reisberg, (see p. 7) and the author leans heavily upon Reisberg's concept related to seven stages of dementia.

When making an assessment of the presence or absence of dementia, the importance of knowing the language used by the sufferer may seem so obvious as to need no comment, but if carers are not present, or, if present, are not asked for information, a false picture of cognitive state may be gained. For example, one may assume that an elderly Italian migrant who has lived in his new country for 30 years will speak the language of the new country. But this may not be so; his language skills will depend on his area of employment, whether he has lived and worked in an enclave of Italian-speaking relatives and friends, and so on.

After a stroke involving aphasia or dysphasia, it is possible for the newly acquired language skills to be lost and older skills to be retained, so that an elderly person whose relatives assume that she speaks/understands English despite her dysphasia may be wrong, and she may have reverted to the language of childhood. Assessment by a speech pathologist must precede any other assessment if there is any doubt as to language and communication skills resulting from brain damage.

Trained health care interpreters are usually available in a well run health care system, but they do need to be "reserved" ahead of time, so that initial enquiries must be made from the carers when an appointment is made for assessment, to find out whether there is a need for preliminary assessment by speech pathologist or attendance at the assessment by a professionally trained health care interpreter. It should be noted that the training is important; one must not rely on staff, professional or domestic, who come from the country in question. The training of interpreters for health work equips them to efface themselves totally from the conversation apart from voicing the words. They maintain the relationship between therapist and patient without intrusion, to the extent that the client and therapist look at each other, and are able to ignore the presence of the interpreter without any conscious effort.

If an untrained person is used, there are very grave risks; the intermediary, for example, may put her own ideas forward as if they came from the client, or may unintentionally change the emphasis of what has been said so that an incorrect picture emerges. Because of the migration programme in Australia, the author has worked through professionally trained health work interpreters on many occasions, and the above comments are the fruit of experience!

One matter which may be crucial to the reliability of assessments of demented persons, but which is often overlooked, is that of visual fields. These may be impaired simply by faulty vision, lack of the correct glasses for the assessment situation, e.g., if reading glasses have been left at home, creating problems when test patterns are to be looked at and copied, objects must be named and their uses described, and so on.

Any defect of vision which reduces the capacity to see print, pictures or objects can affect the outcome of cognitive testing, but cortical blindness, and loss of visual fields because of brain damage, is a still greater problem in assessing dementia.

Persons who have had a car accident, a cortical tumour, a stroke or a series of strokes may well have vision

---

[1]Folstein M.F., Folstein S.E. & McHugh P.R. "Mini-mental state: a practical method for grading the cognitive state of patients, for the clinician." *Journal of psych. res.* 1975, **12**, pp 189-198.

in only part of the normal field (hemianopia).
There may also be an agnosia, a complete inability to interpret anything which is seen or touched, so that the function of even a common object such as a hairbrush is not understood. Although, technically, the condition of dementia may not be present, this condition is so disabling as to render independent living impossible, and indeed the condition may mimic dementia to the uninformed.

Unless assessment of visual fields has been made by a professional orthoptist before any other assessment has been made, the interviewer may tend towards a diagnosis of dementia when, in fact, the answers to questions are affected by the restricted area of vision or by cortical blindness.

Information from the orthoptist should be routinely available to all therapists, music or otherwise, because we need to know about visual field losses in placing people in groups, where to stand to talk to them. We need to know also whether it is considered that the neglect is amenable to improvement or not, which will determine whether we deliberately encourage the patient to look towards the "lost" side or whether we accept the loss as permanent and take it into consideration when we organise music activities and therapy.

Hearing assessment is equally important; a patient who has misheard a question will answer what he thinks he has heard, and if the interviewer is unaware of the deafness, wrong conclusions may be drawn as to cognitive status.

Home Assessment

Professor Tom Arie (Professor of Health Care of the Elderly at Nottingham, U.K.), when visiting Australia in 1984, made it clear to all his listeners that there are grave dangers in assessments done in hospital offices, rather than in the home. The frail, elderly person who has fears that the memory is not as reliable as it used to be, who is probably thereby terrified of being categorised as "demented," is going to be so adversely affected by anxiety that he or she is likely to make all manner of mistakes, appear to be confused and generally below normal cognitively.

Sometimes the office assessment is unavoidable because it is part of a battery of tests such as CAT scans, blood chemistry, orthoptic assessment and so on, which necessarily take place in a hospital or clinic where the equipment and personnel are together. In these circumstances it is the responsibility of the whole team to put at ease both the client and the carer who accompanies him, explaining what is to happen even if it seems probable that the patient will not really understand. But the attitude is understood, the attitude which says, "You are an adult and I will treat you as such," rather than the attitude which says clearly, "You are senile and couldn't understand even if I told you, so I won't bother."

Even though the office assessment may be necessary, any decisions as to placements MUST be backed up by home visits, by two or more of the team, because people usually function far better at home in their familiar surroundings where they are relaxed and comfortable than they do in the office.

Home visits also permit the team to match up their hospital observations, and the patient's statements about her own capacity to look after herself, with the reality of the home. For instance someone may say, "I look after myself well, I buy food from the corner shop and I can certainly go home." But a home visit reveals a refrigerator full of rotting food - which has clearly been there for many months (in one such case, the floor was an obstacle-course of saucepans full of putrid food), or totally empty cupboards, even when the admission was a crisis situation rather than an admission planned far in advance, which could explain the empty cupboards.

One may also see signs of the dangers of memory loss - faeces on the floor, burn marks on walls where electric heaters have set fire to curtains, and so on. At the other end of the scale, a home visit may reveal a better picture than had been estimated, as with a person who was alleged to be mentally ill because he said people were looking at him through the windows of his upper floor apartment. A home assessment revealed that the outside of his apartment building was a mass of scaffolding and it was found that the local boys thought it was amusing to climb up and make faces through the windows at the people inside.

The music therapist should also be encouraged to make home visits for assessment for the same reasons. One such visit proved of enormous value in contributing to the total picture of relationships between husband (carer) and wife (dementing person). By visiting the home, it became clear that the husband's anxiety caused him to be overprotective so that his wife was functioning at a lower level of independence than was imposed by her dementing process.

This had been suspected in hospital visits, but there had been several doubts as to whether it was coming to the hospital which made the husband as well as the wife nervous. A home visit for music therapy, in which the two people were able to relax completely and truly be themselves, revealed greater reserves of competence in the wife than had been suspected. The weekly visits over a matter of three months facilitated two things:

- Trying to determine whether his overprotectiveness was filling a need in himself; if that had been so, it would have been very hard to effect a change.
- When the capacity of the wife had been assessed, it was possible to reassure the husband about letting his wife do things when she wished to do so.

These visits were an interesting demonstration of the overlap between assessment and therapy. Initially the visits were for therapy for both husband and wife, to help them cope with loss and sadness, but also developed into an assessment situation before returning to a (different) therapy basis of encouraging social interaction and building upon the strengths of the relationship.

The reports on what had been observed in these home visits by the music therapist also contributed to the decision-making process about the use of community day-care facilities for the wife, and the support which was required to give the husband courage to allow his wife to stay independently at the day centre while he had a day of being alone to do the things he needed to do. Teamwork is essential in the assessment, care giving and ultimate placement of the dementing person, for the sake of patient and carer alike.

We have already seen that depression may compound dementia and, in some instances, lead to a misdiagnosis of organic dementia rather than pseudo-dementia. In any assessment, whether in office or in the home, it is important to check with the carers for any life events which appear to be linked causally in time with the onset of the cognitive deterioration. In many instances there has been a recent death or major loss - death of the spouse or significant other, loss of independence in leaving the erstwhile matrimonial home to live in a nursing home or with a relative in unfamiliar surroundings, major acquired physical disability such as amputation, and so on. Or there may have been a gradual increase in sadness and loss of spirits, coinciding with cognitive failure and increased frailty.

The carers (often, but not always, family members) are frequently keenly aware of the emotional problems of their apparently-dementing relative, and can describe clearly the changes in behaviour which they have observed.

If it appears likely that we are seeing either a picture which is a combination of dementia and depressive illness, or a condition which arises solely from depressive illness, then psychiatric help should be sought in an effort to alleviate the unhappiness, and in this the music therapist has a special part to play. (See chapter in *Grieving* [2]).

McLean's review article[3] on difficulties in assessment, especially regarding differential diagnosis, is helpful in this matter.

We must also bear in mind that depression and dementia can co-exist, and we must try to deal with the depression, not merely accepting it as untreatable, or the inevitable outcome of the organic dementing process.

In a 1986 article in *The British Journal of Psychiatry*, Robinson[4], of Johns Hopkins Hospital, describes

---

[2]Bright R. *Grieving*. MMB Music Inc., St Louis, USA, 1986. Chapter 11.

[3]McLean S. "Assessing dementia, Part I: difficulties, definitions and differential diagnosis." *Australia and New Zealand jnl. psychiatry*, 1987, **21**, pp 142-174

[4]Robinson R.G. et al "Depression influences intellectual impairment in stroke patients. *British jnl. psychiatry* 1986, **148**, pp 541-547.

how depression influences intellectual functioning following strokes, and since some dementias result from cerebrovascular accidents, it seems reasonable to extrapolate to some extent these findings. We should consider how far the cognitive functioning of our demented patients is adversely affected by their depression, and how far their functioning may be improved, as Robinson recommends, by appropriate doses of antidepressants.

It may be that a specific event or change in life style has been the cause of the concommitant depression, i.e. that we are seeing a reactive depression which is a logical and reasonable response to life events. It may also be something in which we can hope to effect change.

On the other hand, it may be a generalised depression, seen in a person with a long history of major depressive illnesses. But, whichever it is, we must work with our colleagues to distinguish between the deterioration of function due to the organic dementia and that which is due to the depressive illness.

We must not ignore the possibility of suicide even in the apparently demented frail and elderly patient. The author has known three such successful suicides, by people who were aware of their own gradual deterioration, as well as other potential suicides who - given the strength, means and opportunity to carry out their wishes - would probably also have been successful in self-killing.

One of the major difficulties in assessing the presence or absence of depression is that the measuring instruments which are commonly used for estimating depression, such as the Hamilton rating scale[5], depend for their scoring system on the respondent's answers to questions about his feelings, activities and so on. In the presence of dementia it is not possible to gain precise answers to questions because of cognitive losses as well as possible dysphasia. We must therefore depend only on observations of behaviour.

A most useful rating scale has been devised at Cornell University, USA, concerned with these problems of depression in the presence of dementia[6], and the rating is done entirely on the basis of the carer's observations. I am grateful to Dr Alexopoulos, from Cornell Medical Center, New York Hospital, for permission to quote from and to discuss this scale as well as to use it clinically.

The rating scale has been carefully investigated for rater reliability, sensitivity, specificity, and has been compared with the Hamilton rating scale for depression, proving to be better able to differentiate the depression into four groups according to diagnostic criteria.

It looks at all relevant aspects of behaviour, as observed by carers:

- Mood related signs - anxious behaviour, sad behaviour, lack of response to surroundings, and irritability.
- Behavioral disturbance - agitation, retardation, multiple physical complaints, loss of interest (i.e. less involved than previously in daily activities).
- Physical signs - appetite loss, weight loss, lack of energy.
- Cyclic functions - diurnal mood variation, difficulty in falling asleep, multiple wakenings, early morning awakening.

Ideational disturbance - suicide, self-deprecation, pessimism, mood-congruent delusions.

This rating system has several uses; it will assist the physician in his treatment of depression by whatever means seem appropriate. The assessment is likely to lead to greater efforts in psycho-social approaches in an attempt to alleviate the sadness, by whatever means are available, and depending on the level of functioning of the individual. Thus some sufferers are helped by music sessions which lead to increased self-esteem; many are helped by reassurance as to the nature of dementia, that it is an illness which can strike anyone and is in no way the sufferer's fault

---

[5]Hamilton M.A. "A rating scale for depression." *Jnl. of neurol., neurosurg. & psychiatry*, 1960, **40**, pp 56-62.

[6]Alexopoulos G.S., Abrams R.C., Young R.C. & Shamoian C.A. Cornell scale for depression in dementia. New research section, annual meeting of the American psychiatric association, Dallas, 1985.

This need for reassurance must never be rejected as useless, or overlooked, even when we are working with people who appear to have no verbal capacity at all. Even if there is no apparent capacity for sensible conversation, one should offer this reassurance. In this there is an analogy with talking to the unconscious person who has suffered a stroke or other brain damage or who is at the point of death.

Results of the depression rating scale will also assist in the day-to-day programmes for the client, by helping nursing staff and all therapists to have realistic understanding of the mental anguish suffered by a person even with advanced dementia. The phrase sometimes used to describe the wandering demented patient, "The Happy Wanderer," appears to be totally unrelated to the experience of the patient himself, and is probably one of the defence mechanisms used by all of us from time to time when facing a situation of intolerable stress and sadness, that we try to convince ourselves that the patient IS happy, however deteriorated he may appear.

The assessment will also help us to have realistic expectations of what the patient will be able to do, and to hope for improvement if the depression can be ameliorated somewhat. Some of the improvement in patients when they come into hospital after a long time of isolation and deprivation at home can probably be explained by the lifting of depression because of treatment and the positive attitude of staff, as well as by the improved nutritional intake. And the lifting of depression as well as improvements to dementia may be due in part to nutritional intake, because deficiency of folic acid, common in isolated elderly people who are failing to eat an adequate diet, can contribute to both depression and dementia[7].

It is also helpful to have an assessment of cognitive function when we are working with persons who have alcohol-related brain damage, since dysfunction may be extreme, and loss of insight may lead to difficulties in self-rating, so that a system which depends only upon observation by carers is of value.

Persons who are aphasic as the result of a stroke are similarly unsuitable for estimation of depression by any scale which depends upon the subject's comprehension of questions, and on the ability to process and communicate the answers to those questions. For this reason, the author is working with a speech pathologist colleague using the Cornell scale in order to determine the outcome of work in music-speech therapy, on the assumption that lessening of depression indicates a favourable result.

In our observations of changes in behaviour in our elderly clients, all members of the team need to be aware of drug-induced dementia. One such lady was being discussed at a case intake meeting when her medication list was read out, and a member of the team noticed that the list included two brand names for the same digitalis preparation, so that - by a failure in communication between her cardiologist and her family physician about her prescriptions - she was taking double the correct dose of digitalis, and it was found that her dementia was explained by this intoxication. Her admission to hospital was therefore undertaken with a plan which was very different from what had been envisaged when the investigation of the causes of her dementia had been expected to be a major issue.

We need also to be aware of changes in family situations, which can cause a change in mental status to a previously stable elderly person. The music therapist, who so often works in the family milieu even in a hospital setting, will often be aware of, for example, the relocation of a middle-aged son to another State, the death of a beloved grandchild, fears over a daughter's health when she is suddenly admitted to hospital, and so on.

Such observations form an important part of our on-going assessment. Assessment is not a once-only activity but must be maintained on a day-by-day basis, even if only on an informal level, and - as noted on page 19 - we need to note in writing the results of our observations and assessment.

In working with the elderly and/or demented client, we are unlikely to produce sheet after sheet of paper giving personality profiles, and elaborate aims and objectives for therapy, no matter what our field of work. What we must do is to use our ears, our eyes, our hands and even our noses to assess the continually-changing status of our patients, the state of their skin and hair (looking out for hypothyroid problems), the smell of their clothes if they are incontinent, looking out for the mown-hay smell which is the

[7]Hyams D.E. "The blood." *Textbook of geriatric medicine and gerontology,* (ed. Brocklehurst), Churchill-Livingstone, Edinburgh & London, 1973, p 563

characteristic smell associated with diabetes, and so on.

General Summary

What behaviours and physical signs should guide us as we assess people for dementia and its consequences? The following list is a first guide in our observations, and we shall find that we change it or expand it as our experience grows.

- In meeting people on several occasions, do they have any recollection, when reminded, of having met us before or is each encounter a totally new experience?
  The matter of "when reminded" is important because benign memory loss can lead us to forget temporarily a previous meeting but it returns to us when we are reminded, whereas in the more significant memory loss of dementia there is total forgetting, even after a reminder has been given.
- Can the patient join in the singing of music which, one assumes, was familiar to him from times past?
- If given an instrument such as a Bongo drum, does he have any idea of what it is, how to use it?
- Similarly with a triangle and beater (a far more complex task)?
- Can he copy movements demonstrated in a mobilisation session?
- Is he aware in any way of other people in the group?
- Is he aware in any way of his surroundings - the weather, the view from the window, etc?
- Does he wander away and, if requested, does he return after a while to re-join the session?
- Is he incontinent of (a) urine (b) faeces?
- Are his movements very slow?
- Does he seem unhappy and tearful over specific stimuli such as a particular song or piece of music, or is his sadness all-pervasive?
- Can he describe to you how he feels if he is tearful and unhappy?
- Do his relatives report any recent losses and griefs which could cause depression?
- Does he have, or has he had in the past, any physical disability which may contribute to apparent or actual dementia, e.g. Parkinson's disease, Huntington's disease, cerebral tumours, brain injury from an accident, transient ischaemic attacks (T.I.A.'s), multiple strokes etc?
- Assessment of drug regimes may seem inappropriate for therapists, but it is of interest to ask what treatment the sufferer has had, e.g. for Parkinson's disease or heart disease, since drug regimes, poorly prescribed or monitored, can cause or exacerbate dementia, and information on this must be passed on to others in the team.
- Does he appear to have visual or auditory hallucinations?
- Does he appear to have delusions of persecution etc?
- Is he (without apparent cause) aggressive towards fellow-patients and/or staff and/or relatives?

The answers to these questions are not usually gathered together on one occasion, but should be assessed informally in the course of two or more sessions, the results collated and added to the clinical notes as well as being presented at a team meeting at which the diagnosis and presentation of dementia is under discussion.

The decision as to whether one scores such assessment numerically is difficult; the overall picture is the most important thing to be gleaned from one's assessment, and it is improbable that there will be a cut-off point, below which the person is to be regarded as unsuitable for music activities. It may, however, be helpful in comparing one client with another, or in assessing any treatment effects, to have numerical scores achieved by collating one's assessments over two or three weeks, as suggested above.

Music Skills Assessment

Basic music skills have already been listed above in the total observations for assessment, and for most music therapy work in advanced dementia, from whatever cause, this list covers all that are required.

The music is used as a means to an end rather than an end in itself. It is used to improve awareness of other people and of the surroundings, to improve self-esteem, give an opportunity for decision-making and freedom of choice, the expression of

feelings of joy or sadness, opportunity for reminiscence, enhancing physical mobility in order to overcome contractures and other disuse syndromes, and so on.

However, there may be instances in which a more accurate assessment of music skills is genuinely needed, as, for instance, when a person has been a professional musician and one wishes to find out whether any use can be made of previous skills in order to enhance present quality of living, or to assess how much of pre-existing skills has been lost as a result of brain damage from a motor vehicle accident, which assessment might well form part of legal proceedings.

The long-established Seashore tests of musical talent[8] depend for much of their rating scores on the ability of the subject to hear a musical excerpt, hold it in the memory and, after listening to a second excerpt, compare certain musical features of the two. Clearly this is at least in part dependent upon intact memory function, and for that reason the tests are totally inappropriate for work with any dementing person since memory failure is one of the main presenting features of the syndrome. In the opinion of the author, any use of the Seashore music tests with older persons must be preceded by assessment of memory function; otherwise there may be no validity in the level of musical talent as rated in the test scores. And in any case, strong doubts have now been thrown upon the validity of the tests with normal subjects.[9]

What can one do instead?

One's tests for the dementing subject are limited by various factors:

1. Short-term memory loss.
2. Reduced concentration span, which can result from depression as well as from dementia.[10]
3. Difficulties with body image, especially when asked to copy a movement or activity, even when it has been clearly demonstrated.
4. Difficulties, to the extreme, in following a sequence of instructions, not only because of memory loss but because of defects in organisational skills.
5. Difficulties with understanding the spoken word.
6. Difficulty in speaking and answering.
7. Difficulties in comprehending the use of objects and of actually using them appropriately if asked to do something, due to agnosia and apraxia.
8. Concomitant sensory losses such as deafness, loss of tactile sensation, loss of visual fields, lateral neglect. (These may be part of the dementia or may arise from an intercurrent problem such as stroke.)

Despite this formidable list, assessment of music skills, in general terms, is not difficult!

The method adopted must be that of the here-and-now, and not "listen to this, remember it and then compare it with that".

We must, however, note that we are not testing MUSICALITY, which bestows a capacity to enjoy listening to music even if all other avenues are closed. All we are testing is MUSIC SKILLS, the capacity to join in with certain music activities. The two are not the same. A subject may score almost nil on the tests given below, and yet still be an appropriate person to attend a music group for simple passive enjoyment and for stimulation, even if no outward response is visible.

NOTE: As with all the tests listed in this section, failure to score well does not necessarily indicate loss of rhythmic or melodic sense but may well indicate simply that one of the problems listed above has supervened. Test anxiety is an additional limiting factor which reduces scoring, especially in early dementia when the subject is frightened about the losses he is experiencing. Always base your opinions on everyday

---

[8]Seashore C.E.(ed) *Measurement of musical talent.* Uni. of Iowa Press, USA, 1935.

[9]Henson R.A. "The performance of professional musicians, on the seashore measures of musical talent: an unexpected finding." *Cortex*, April 1982, **18**, (1), pp 153-157.

[10]Goodwin D.W. et al. *Psychiatric diagnosis.* Oxford University Press, 1979. p 230

observations of behaviour as being of more value than formal testing.

The author believes that the following tests should only be attempted with persons perceived as being in Reisberg's stages 2 or 3. Cognitive and motor planning losses will probably invalidate testing in later stages.

Testing of Rhythmic Skills

Play a strongly rhythmic piece, e.g., march, jig, reel, and invite the subject to tap his feet in time to the music. Observe whether his feet do keep time or whether he fails to respond at all, taps aimlessly etc. Use words which are readily understood - the author, when doing this test once, invited a subject to tap her feet, whereupon she bent over and tapped her fingers on the end of her shoes - indeed "tapping her feet", but not quite what had been expected!

Alternatively, clap hands yourself in time to a record, and observe whether or not the person joins in, and - if so - whether the clapping is in time to the music. (Persons whose brain impairment prevents them from following instructions may yet act appropriately when left to themselves without any verbal directions.)

Without giving any long instructions, and perhaps without any conversation at all (depending on the survival of verbal skills in the patient), one would hand the subject a musical instrument such as a bongo drum (better than a drum which requires drum-sticks, since apraxia may make the use of a tool impossible).

Using a reassuring remark such as "You will know this!" or just a smile, start to play in a brisk tempo, with strong tone and marked accents, a well-known march or other strongly rhythmical tune. The choice of the piece will depend upon the cultural background of the person, elicited in conversation with relatives, in order to find out the ethnic origin, and musical preference. If necessary, one can use a tape or record of this music, and play a bongo drum oneself, observing simply whether the subject starts to beat out the correct rhythm/thumps aimlessly/sits motionless. One can then withdraw from the playing, indicating by voice or gesture "You keep going!" and see whether the subject continues to play his drum.

Nevertheless, it must be recognised that musicality may be masked by brain damage, so that the person who, because of ideational apraxia, sucks a maraca as if it were an ice cream, may yet enjoy listening to music and join in singing quite appropriately. (See below for scoring.)

Next tap out firmly a simple rhythm, and ask the subject to copy it.

Next play on a pitched instrument such as a piano a strong rhythmic pattern such as C, D, E, F, G, G, to dotted rhythm, and invite (by word or gesture) the subject to beat out an answering phrase. [see NOTE above.]

Melody Recognition

Play the national anthem known to the subject and observe responses. Appropriate responses might include: Standing to attention. Saluting. Singing the tune and/or words. A change to a more upright posture and a pleased smile. Crying could also be an appropriate response because of personal associations (e.g., remembering the death of a son in a war), but since lability is also a feature of dementia, the precise implication of crying in response to the national anthem or song is almost impossible to assess with any degree of accuracy.

Other well-known songs can be used similarly, but to assess the significance of results one must check with the family that any given tune was in fact familiar to the person. There is no significance in failing to recognise a tune which you never knew anyway!

Pitch Perception & Execution

Play a well-known melody and invite the subject to sing along with you, whilst you sing too.

Play a well-known melody or a major scale, within the vocal range of the subject, leaving out the final note. By gesture of your hand, indicate that the person is to sing the final note.

One can also assess pitch discrimination by playing a well-known melody with some blatant wrong notes, and observe any facial expression which indicates surprise or pain.

Scoring

(In results, "partially" = an attempt was made but was partly incorrect, "not at all" = an attempt was made but this was totally wrong.)

- Can keep time with music, clapping or tapping feet: perfectly/partially/not at all/no response.
- Can maintain rhythm on drum: perfectly/partially/not at all/no response.
- Can tap or clap, copying given phrase: perfectly/partially/not at all/no response.
- Can play answering rhythm to that played by the tester: perfectly/partially/not at all/no response.

Pitch

- Can sing along with well-known tune [with words included]: perfectly/partially/not at all/no response.
- Can complete musical scale correctly: yes/no/no response.
- Can detect mistakes in well-known tune: all/some/none.

It must be noted that if the subject is an anxious person the total score on these tests may be nil, and yet - in a social group in which the same or similar activities take place - he or she will function perfectly adequately, to her own and other people's satisfaction and pleasure.

For more advanced testing, if it is known that the subject has been a professional musician, then the same tests in a more advanced form are appropriate, but still avoiding skills which depend upon memory. If - for purposes of litigation - one needs to demonstrate the global effects of the brain damage upon the previous music skills, e.g., in dementia following a motor vehicle accident, then the Seashore test battery could be used. **Nevertheless one must not ignore the possibility of a catastrophic response in the subject who - by the use of such a test - becomes aware that all his previous skills have been obliterated.**

The ethics of such testing, as distinct from legal requirements, may lead to ambivalence as to one's role in the matter.

For the music therapist working as a member of a clinical team, the most useful and indeed the most interesting assessment will be the observation of behavioural changes achieved as the result of our work. By one definition, music therapy is the planned use of music to reach non-musical goals, and with this in mind we may see the assessment of behavioural change as far more important than assessment of music skills as such, or of the level of dementia - although this information will help us to plan our programmes for best results.

Thus with dementing persons we are looking for decreases in aggression, wandering, incontinence, and increases in attention span, enjoyment, eating patterns, sleep patterns, optimism etc.

It is difficult to assess many components of behaviour at the one time unless one makes a video tape of the session and then asks two or more independent observers to rate changes in target behaviours which have been nominated beforehand.

The system preferred by the author is to plan a series of six weekly sessions with a programme of target behaviours in mind, videotape each session, and ask independent raters to assess each session. Means are then established for the results. But in many hospitals video work is forbidden because of the statutory requirement that informed consent be given by all patients, even for in-hospital work. Clearly for dementing persons informed consent is not possible.

It must be noted that our work will not be complete in six weeks - one may need to establish a permanent programme - but six weeks may well show whether our intervention is having an effect, and we can then plan ahead with better basis of knowledge.

Target behaviours in which change is fairly readily observed include:

- general alertness and posture.
- tolerance of physical contact from one person to another.
- initiation of physical contact from one person to another.
- in-seat behaviour, how often each person gets up and how long he stays away, and whether he returns readily on request.
- aggressive behaviour.
- participation in e.g. singing, instrumental work.
- communicative speech.
- free physical movement, rhythmic actions as appropriate.

It is also helpful to ask staff opinions as to ward behaviour following a music session, and for how long the improvements last, whether they are generalised to ward behaviour as a whole. It must be recognised that ward staff are not always identical in the extent to which they notice changes or see a causal relationship between the behaviour they observe and the recent participation in a music therapy session.

A nurse who supervised the coffee break which followed music group noted that patients with early or moderate dementia interacted more socially after the group than was observed in the waiting room before the therapy session.

Sometimes the physical effects and psychological effects last for some time. In one instance, the domiciliary nurse, visiting the home of a demented client who attended music from time to time, was always able to tell when he had been to music the day before because of the lessening of his physical rigidity and his free-er conversation. Such evidence is anecdotal and yet is none the less important.

The therapist will have to decide whether to establish a set list of target behaviours for all dementing persons, or whether it is better to prepare a separate programme for each individual. One approach is to analyse which positive behaviours one wishes to encourage and which negative behaviours one wishes to discourage, assess each client to see how he rates on these, and prepare an individually-tailored programme of music involvement to fit his needs. Although this is in one sense a behaviour modification approach, it must never be planned "mechanically", but must take into account the musical taste and preference of the client, his stage of deterioration, his emotional state, his resources, his family support and so on.

General Record Keeping

It is essential that we keep accurate records of what is found in assessment as well as achieved in everyday therapy thereafter. If we do not keep records, then we are not therapists but recreationists! Some music therapists keep only their own records, but this is less helpful than if we contribute to the patient's general clinical files, so that our work goes hand-in-hand with that of other professionals who are involved in care, for mutual benefit.

The Problem Orientated Medical Record (P.O.M.R.) system is well-suited to work in music therapy.[11] It provides us with a concise method of noting our objective observations, followed by our notes on what the patient reports subjectively (in dementia, probably very little), followed by our treatment plans and goals. The Data Base at the beginning of the record contains our initial assessment, and those of us who work in places where P.O.M.R. is the system in use find it helpful to include the precis of our music therapy assessment in the Data Base so that it is there for reference by all clinical staff.

---

[11] Petrie J.C. & McIntyre N. *The problem orientated medical record.* Churchill-Livingstone, New York, 1977.

Also included at the beginning of the file is a Problem List, on which each problem is noted and numbered, including the date at which it was first observed, followed by a brief outline of the management plan, and a space for noting when the problem was considered to be at an end. (In dementia, this may never occur.) Differential diagnoses would appear in the Data Base, so that for a person with suspected organic dementing process, there will be a note of, for example, "D.D.: hypothyroid, major depressive illness, illness, Folic Acid deficiency ?" with tests which were performed to exclude these and the results.

The problem lists may then appear thus:

Problem	Date noted	Management	Resolved
• Alzheimer Dementia	21/7/85	Affirmative R.O. (Reality Orientation).	
• Contractures of knees	21/7/86	Physiotherapy	
• Depression	26/7/86	Music Therapy. Family conference. Doxepin.	
• Incontinence Bladder only	2/8/86	2-hourly toileting. Mid-stream urine sample, test for bacteria in urine. (Drug prescribed)	5/8/86
• Night-time waking	12/8/86	Full day programme of stimulation & activity	26/8/86

When writing in the body of the files, one then puts into the margin the problem number, which makes it easy for staff who need to find particular items of treatment and outcome to identify the pages on which those matters are discussed, rather than ploughing through the entire file.

The convention is that one does not write up each and every treatment session, but makes notes only when there has been some change.

These concise notes can be supplemented with one's own files which give detailed accounts of what has been done, and more detailed lists of goals and objectives. In working with dementing persons, the goals are necessarily restricted by the nature of the expected deterioration, but ameliorating the impact of the process upon sufferer and family is a legitimate aim of one's programmes.

ASSESSMENT - A SUMMARY

When working in dementia, it is important to remember that our assessment is functional, i.e. it seeks to assess the client's status in order to see how much of the condition is reversible, to plan more effective treatment, more appropriate placement, and to facilitate better relationships between sufferer and family as well as between the sufferer and his world.

We need also to remember that appearances can be deceptive. For instance, we may see a person with strong facial grimaces - tardive dyskinesia - and assume from this that he or she is unsuitable for inclusion in music sessions apart from the most basic kind. But in fact this dyskinesia is present in some of the normal population, and is also seen in persons who have, over a long period of time, had to take either neuroleptic drugs or anti-Parkinsonian medication.[12] It is not necessarily correlated

[12] Chacko R. C. et al "Prevalence of tardive dyskinesia in geropsychiatric outpatients". *Jnl. Clin. Psychiat.*, 1985, (Feb) **46** (2), pp 55 - 57.

with dementia. Only with meticulous personal observation of behaviour can we be certain of the correctness of our assessment.

On-going assessment goes hand in hand with programme planning, it is not an end in itself, and programme planning is enhanced by good record-keeping.

We must be certain that we work as humanitarian pragmatists, and that we retain the good of the patient as our prime goal. We may nevertheless at the same time hope to gain solid research results in order to help other people and extend the value of our innovative work.

CHAPTER 3

HOW MUSIC THERAPY HELPS DEMENTING PERSONS - I

In planning any group activity, one may have to meet the challenge of the mixed group.

This may be in a nursing home where some people in a ward are dementing whilst others are suffering from physical frailty only. It may be in a psychiatric hospital where, in a psycho-geriatric ward, there is likely to be a mixture of clients, some suffering from Alzheimer-type dementia, some from late-onset psychiatric illness, some from the sequelae of strokes or motor-vehicle accident brain damage, some from Korsakov's psychosis or other alcohol-related brain damage which necessitates institutional care, and some older persons with Down's syndrome.

This challenge may be solved by separating the clients into small groups, which in any case give us the best method of working. But this is not always possible, and the mixed levels of functioning can create problems. In one such group, the author was offering percussion instruments to some of the participants, and offered a most costly set of metal chime bars in a leather case to a lady who was known to be relatively alert and interested. She looked up in horror and said, in tones of sarcasm and disgust, "I'm not in my second childhood YET, thank you very much!"

Programmes need to be planned in such a way that those who are alert do not feel humiliated and those who are aware of their own deficiencies do not feel pressured. Music is perhaps one of the few media through which such compromises can be achieved, in that music can be enjoyed at different levels at the same time by different members of a group. For example, some can listen to a Chopin waltz simply as a pretty tune, whilst others can visualise the ballet in which the tune was used, or think about the life of the composer and the influence of his national heritage upon his composition.

In instrumental work, some members of a group, who are cognitively intact and only frail physically, can play complex rhythms from a chart whilst others, who are dementing, provide a "ground bass" of regular drum beats.

Simple folk-dancing can be enjoyed as an interesting sequence by the non-demented elderly people whilst the dementing participants clap their hands in time with the music.

And so on.

But it must be acknowledged that one can work far more effectively if one can separate the dementing clients from the others, for the greater benefit of all. One's planning and sense of purpose is severely curtailed if one has to work in a mixed group where no real therapeutic aims can be achieved, and for the remainder of this booklet it will be assumed that separation according to functional level is possible.

(i) Self-esteem and the Lessening of Depression

Our aim should be to impart to the sufferer some sense of:

- Competence - we need to provide an activity in which it is possible for the sufferer to experience a measure of success.
- Individuality - interactions with the sufferer should emphasise his identity, always treating him as an individual and never merely as "One of the dements in room...."
- Opportunity either for verbalising his own feelings about helplessness and loss, or saying things for him if he is unable to express them himself. There is no risk of "putting ideas into his head by doing this;" the feelings are certainly there, and by expressing them in an empathic manner we should be able to bring relief and not anguish.

How does music come into this?

As we have already seen, music-based therapy is using old memory traces which are intact, and we can therefore often reach those who are otherwise inaccessible. But there is still a need for careful planning based upon knowledge of both the pathology and the person - the extent to which his dementing process has advanced and his previous life-history and preferences.

For the person with early dementia, it is often possible for him to express a preference, especially if cues are given. It has been shown that cuing is of value in retrieval from the memory[1], and cuing can be adapted, depending on the degree of dementia present. (See below for additional discussion.) For example, an early sufferer may respond to the question "What is your favorite tune?" by giving the title and then joining in when the tune is played, by singing, moving in time with the music, playing an instrument and so on. But for another person, it will be necessary to give a simple cue "Your wife tells me you used to enjoy dancing and that the waltz was your favorite - do you remember that one you used to dance with her?" An additional cue in this sequence may be necessary for some, by having the opening words given, or the beginning of the melody.

For another person, whose tastes were towards "classical" music, by playing an excerpt of Beethoven, Mozart - or whoever was the favoured composer - further ideas may be elicited, but for a person with more advanced dementia, a further cue will be necessary - "Do you like this tune by Brahms, I believe he was your best-loved composer?" Then play the Brahms Lullaby, or any other excerpt which the person was known to have liked.

We should note that to hear the familiar music from the past may elicit happiness and tears together; as one non-dementing person expressed it: "The memory itself is a happy one but you are sad because it IS only a memory."

The precise level of cuing depends on the cognitive state of the individual; for the early sufferer the music alone may be sufficient, but for others verbal cues of varying complexity will be required.

For example, an early sufferer may be shown a bunch of Spring flowers and - when asked - will probably be able to suggest pieces of music which are linked with Spring: Mendelssohn's Spring Song, *Springtime in the Rockies, It might as well be Spring, Spring will be a little late this year,* etc. For a person in a more advanced stage, one will need to give a stronger cue - "Do you know that song - 'When it's Springtime in .....' and he will probably be able to complete the title by saying, "In the Rockies", whereas a person with still more advanced dementia may need almost the whole title, leaving only the final syllable to complete. But for all such examples, the person is given a sense of achievement and success because we have geared our cues to the individual's level of functioning.

The passing around of objects, as described in Chapter 4 on social awareness and re-orientation, also constitutes a cue, and contributes to the sense of success and competence experienced by the sufferer.

In using music to address severe depression and loss of self-esteem we are usually working at an individual level, at least in the first instance, but the methods used will be virtually identical with those used in group work for social awareness.

The main objectives are to impart a sense of success, in the recognition of loved music and of individuality, through our one-to-one approach as well as in the music we provide. Through the individual approach we shall also have an opportunity for simple counselling and the making of positive statements as to the personal worth of the client. We must acknowledge that these may be apparently forgotten from day to day, but the lift to the spirits which our work imparts is of value nonetheless.

(ii) Aggressive Behaviour and Wandering

Staff burn-out is a topic which receives much attention today, and and it seems safe to assume that the more stressful the patients' behaviour, the more likelihood there is of staff burn-out. In 1985 the author conducted a small-scale investigation in order to find out which behaviours in "difficult-to-manage" demented persons caused most stress in institutional staff, and also how staff viewed the possible uses of music in reducing that stress.

[I am grateful for the editorial policy of the journal "The Clinical Gerontologist" which permits me to reproduce here the main substance of an article published in that journal, which summed up the results of

---

[1]Diesfeldt H.F.A. "The importance of encoding instructions and retrieval cues in the assessment of memory in senile dementia" *Arch. Geront. Geriatr.*, 1984, 3, pp 51-57

the survey mentioned above.]

Over some 25 years, nurses have commented to the present author that even demented patients respond to music, and that their behaviour is not only "better" (more tolerable to staff?) during the music session but that there appears often to be some degree of carry-over into general ward behaviour for a time afterwards.

In order to investigate this, it was decided to find out which behaviours are most difficult for nursing staff to cope with, and then to see how music therapy may be used most effectively. Styles of intervention are discussed, to see which are the most helpful in achieving personal satisfaction for the patients, and also for improving everyday ward atmosphere for staff and patients through the music-based relationships.

This paper is the outcome of that investigation and is presented here almost completely even though it duplicates a number of comments made elsewhere in this monograph.

Manageable or Unmanageable?

In general, those who work with demented patients tend to concentrate on their positive attributes and their pleasanter personality traits rather than on the problems. In view, however, of the incidence of staff burn-out, it is also important that we do consider from time to time the difficulties which are experienced, even if only in order to devise ways of minimising them.

The concepts of manageable, unmanageable or difficult-to-manage are, in practical terms, a relative matter only. For example, a person with only a moderate impairment may be considered to be unmanageable at home if she lives alone and has a degree of memory loss such that she is likely to leave a pan of hot fat on the stove and set fire to the house, forget that she has taken medication such as a digitalis preparation and take a second dose (resulting in toxicity), or if there is a degree of paranoia such that the door is barred against Meals on Wheels (and nutrition is compromised). On the other hand, someone with these problems would present only minimal difficulty if he or she were living under appropriate supervision in a frail aged hostel. Extremely difficult behaviour is seen in the incontinent man with violent aggression towards anyone who approaches him, who would be regarded as unmanageable by relatives at home, or in a nursing home where there is a low staffing ratio, but would be regarded only as "difficult to manage" in a hospital with adequate staffing levels, where two people can distract or restrain him from violence whilst a third person changes his wet pyjamas.

The person being cared for at home may cause so much distress to the family that he or she is regarded as "impossible to keep at home" (i.e. unmanageable) if the behaviour is emotionally intolerable. Greene and colleagues[2] described the behaviour which carers in the home find stressful, and noted that what is commonly perceived as stressful is the change in the relative from an active, involved person to a withdrawn and isolated person, with marked changes of mood. And yet a nurse, who is emotionally uninvolved, may not be so distressed by the changes. Perhaps there is a parallel here with responses noted in relatives of head injury patients[3]. Bodily change is relatively easy to accept, and what is most difficult to adapt to is the change in personality.

We can, however, look at manageability in terms of staff stress within institutions, and it is this aspect which was considered in this investigation.

"Stress" is used here in the everyday common usage of the word, rather than in Selye's concept of useful stress which helps us to mature[4].

When we consider the stress experienced by staff in caring for those suffering from dementia, we may think of stressful sensory stimuli that are experienced. We are affected by sound, e.g. from patients who shout frequently, or constantly grumble and complain, from constant verbal abuse, from constant crying. We are affected also through our sense of smell - from incontinence of faeces and urine, and the other body odours that cannot always be removed. We are affected through the sense of touch when we have to clear up

[2]Greene J.G. et al. "Measuring behavioural disturbance in elderly demented patients in the community and its effects on relatives. A factor analytic study." *Age & ageing*. 1982, **11**, pp 121-126.

[3]Proctor H. Head injuries. *Physiotherapy*, December, 1973, 59, (12) **10**, pp 380-382.

[4]Selye H. *Stress without distress*. Hodder & Stoughton, U.K., 1975, p. 31.

stained clothes and bed linen, and through sight, e.g. when we have to see table manners that revolt us, clothes stained with food, disinhibited sexual behaviour, trails of faeces along the floor where an incontinent patient has walked, and so on. These all overlap with psychosocial stress, as also do situations where we observe and try to prevent verbal and physical abuse by a violent patient towards fellow residents, when we try to persuade patients to take life-preserving medication or drink adequate fluids, try to keep within the ward a person who is constantly trying to escape to "get home to feed the baby", etc.

We may also suffer from loss of self-esteem, in itself a stressful experience, because of our inability keep things running smoothly, and from the accusations - however groundless - which may be levelled at us by angry or paranoid patients.

The extent to which we are able to cope may be altered by our attitudes and also by our social support systems, although this is somewhat a matter for conjecture. There is also a suggestion that Type A personalities are more at risk of stress than are Type B people[5].

If the perfectionist is indeed more at risk of stress than the easy-going person, this may well explain some of the stress of work with the demented, where cleanliness, planning, neatness and timetables are impossible to achieve without undue pressure being placed upon both patients and staff, and where the unforeseeable is the rule!

Finding Out About Staff Stress

No attempt was made to measure harmful stress physiologically. It was decided that the subjective perceptions of the staff about their own degree of stress were more important in this particular context than any attempt to prove or disprove objectively the correctness of these perceptions. If one FEELS stressed, then one probably IS stressed[6]!

A questionnaire was drawn up after consultation with nurses at a variety of levels, who were asked what kind of behaviour caused them to feel that they were suffering from stress. The behaviours suggested were then collated, and overlapping suggestions were combined as accurately as possible, in order to prevent the questionnaire being impossibly long. Two sections (B & D of the questionnaire), concerned with personal ways of coping with stress, produced such diverse results, without any immediately obvious statistical significance of association, that they have been omitted here.

In drawing up the questionnaire, it was hypothesised that the level of nursing or other education might be one factor affecting stress, in that coping with difficult behaviour could perhaps be easier for the highly educated (registered) staff member who understands the reasons for the behaviours. Respondents were therefore asked to give their professional status. Preliminary consideration of the data does not support the hypothesis.

On the other hand, the extent to which one is held responsible for patients' well-being might be more of a a source of stress to registered staff compared with unregistered, since it is the Registered Nurses who normally carry the ultimate responsibility. Again, preliminary consideration of data does not support this hypothesis. Some of the highest and some of the lowest individual stress totals were reported both by Directors of Nursing, and by Nursing Aides who have little or no formal training and no heavy burden of legal liability.

Morale of a unit was also seen as a possible modifying factor, in that an individual working in a unit which lacks good team morale may experience more stress than a person who works with supportive colleagues. There does appear to be a difference in reported stress from one unit to another, but whether this is due to team morale or some other factor is not yet certain.

Respondents were asked to fill in replies to a section concerned with the actual music activities in their unit. It was known that none of the units has a full music THERAPY programme, but that - depending on individual talents, time and interests - some music activities probably took place, even if this was only a

---

[5]Tennant C. et al. "The concept of stress." *Australia and New Zealand journal of psychiatry*, June 1985, **19** (2), pp 113-119.
[6]Wyatt A. "Occupational stress." *Jnl. occ. health & safety*, Aust. & N.Z., 1985, **1**, (1), pp 6-9.

matter of selection of an appropriate radio station.

The questionnaire was administered informally to staff working in two types of establishments in which persons suffering from advanced dementia are cared for: psycho-geriatric units and nursing homes. Four of the units were in a large State institution and, of the nursing homes, three were Church-run establishments where there are substantial numbers of dementia sufferers, and one unit was a privately-run nursing home with special interests in, and programmes for, dementia sufferers.

Post-graduate students in two Gerontological Nursing courses also filled out the questionnaire, all of these subjects being Registered Nurses.

Most patients being cared for by respondents to the questionnaire suffered from Alzheimer's disease or dementia of the Alzheimer type, but there were also some with:

- Multi-infarct dementia.
- Dementia following a single stroke.
- Parkinsonian dementia.
- Huntington's disease.
- Late-onset schizophrenia and other psychiatric illnesses.
- Psychotic depression with organic features.
- Extreme neurotic depression.
- Brain damage resulting from head injuries.
- Alcohol-related brain damage with dementia.
- Dementia of advanced Down's syndrome.
- A combination of two or more of these.

The Questionnaire

MUSIC THERAPY AND THE DIFFICULT-TO-MANAGE DEMENTED PATIENT

Part A

There are various behaviours which lead staff to see patients as "difficult", and one way of estimating the degree of difficulty in management seems to be to measure the perception of stress caused by their behaviours. Printed below is a list of behaviours, and you are asked to rate them for the amount of stress YOU PERSONALLY experience according to the following 5-point rating scale:

0 = causes me no stress.
1 = causes me a little stress.
2 = causes me moderate stress.
3 = causes me considerable stress.
4 = causes me intolerable stress.

Behaviour	Rating
1. Verbally aggressive behaviour to staff.	
2. Physically aggressive behaviour to staff.	
3. Verbally aggressive behaviour to fellow-patients.	
4. Physically aggressive behaviour to fellow-patients.	
5. Shouting, generally noisy behaviour.	
6. Grumbling, complaining, accusations.	
7. Incontinence of urine.	
8. Incontinence of faeces.	
9. Overt sexual behaviour, masturbation in public.	
10. Refusing to eat meals.	
11. Refusing to drink.	
12. Refusing to take medication.	
13. Refusing to co-operate in ward programme.	
14. Constant efforts to leave ward/unit.	
15. Repeated confused questioning.	

Behaviour	**Rating**
16. Interfering with other people's property.	
17. Greedy behaviour, trying to steal food.	
18. Messy eating, food on clothes.	
19. Day/night reversal.	
20. Constant crying & sadness.	

Part B is omitted here, for reasons stated above.

Part C

I use music to help me cope with patients in various ways:

1. Singing with patients as I get them dressed.....
2. Singing with patients as we walk along......
3. Choosing a radio station that plays the kind of music the patients like....
4. Putting on tapes or records of the kind of music that is familiar to them.......
5. Talking to them individually about memories connected with music......
6. Talking to the patients in a group about memories connected with music.......
7. Using music to enhance exercise programmes......
8. Helping to organise singalongs etc..............
9. Using percussion instruments for music sessions......
10. Using music to enhance other programmes, e.g. Reality Orientation, Quiz, Newspaper sessions.......
11. Using music to distract those who are angry/upset etc.......
12. Other...

Part D omitted here, to be discussed below.

What Was Found Out

Behaviour/Stress Tables

A hundred and eleven questionnaires were completed; of the subjects, 59 were Registered Nurses, 45 were unregistered nurses, and seven subjects were involved in non-nursing duties such as podiatry and recreation, but were in close contact with patients.

Stress rating was measured by totalling the stress ratings recorded for the 20 behaviours listed. The possible range was from 0 - 80, actual range 1 - 50.

Mean for the entire population	24.88
Standard deviation	12.63
Ratio of mean to standard deviation	1.97

Hence, the degree of confidence that the behaviours listed are, on the whole, stressful exceeds 95%. (We are looking at only one "tail" of the frequency distribution.)

Individual Behaviours

(Please refer back to the list in Part A above.)

Behaviour	Mean	Stand. Dev.	Ratio
4	2.468	1.016	2.43
2	1.937	1.064	1.82
20	1.667	0.994	1.68
14	1.604	1.114	1.68
3	1.559	0.997	1.56
5	1.432	1.076	1.33

Behaviour	Mean	Stand. Dev.	Ratio
16	1.297	0.940	1.38

Above this line, it is reasonable to assume that the behaviours are generally productive of stress in hospital/nursing home nursing staff, in that they are significantly different from zero at the 90% confidence level.

Behaviour	Mean	Stand. Dev.	Ratio
9	1.288	1.238	1.04
1	1.270	1.044	1.22
6	1.207	1.019	1.18
11	1.099	1.026	1.07
15	1.072	1.024	1.05
12	1.063	1.021	1.04
19	0.963	1.017	0.95
10	0.882	0.922	0.96
8	0.774	0.891	0.87
18	0.676	0.906	0.75
13	0.613	0.777	0.79
7	0.405	0.652	0.62

From the spread of scores we may conclude that perceived stress varies from one person to another, and that there must be factors influencing this. No conclusion can at present be drawn as to what these factors are.

The behaviours in which respondents perceived themselves as having lower stress varied as to category, but No 9 (overt sexual behaviour, masturbation in public) is interesting in that the figures reflect what had been expected - that this is a highly individual matter. It is a behaviour which distresses some staff greatly, but leaves others entirely unperturbed.

The one behaviour which was given a positive stress rating by all respondents was No 4, physical aggression to fellow-patients. The figures are significant well above the 95% confidence level. Presumably the carer is stressed by the unpredictability of the behaviour and the feeling of personal helplessness, together with empathy for the helplessness of the patient who is attacked. Incontinence was rated low, and one may speculate that this is because it is something which is readily dealt with by nursing staff.

Staff Music Activities

The frequency of each music activity carried out by nurses are listed below:

Activity	Frequency
3. Choosing the radio station to suit patients' preferences.	98
4. Putting on recordings to suit patients' preferences.	89
5. Talking individually about associations with music.	64
2. Singing with patients as you walk along.	59
1. Singing as patients are dressed in the morning.	57
11. Using music to distract those who are angry, upset.	57
6. Talking with groups about associations with music.	51
7. Using music to enhance exercises	50
8. Singalongs.	49
10. Using music in quizzes, reality orientation, etc.	23
9. Percussion instrument work.	22
12. Other	9

No 12, "Other" included religious music for services, music for dancing, concerts by staff or visitors.

Part D of the questionnaire was concerned with attitudes to music, whether or not it helped nursing staff to feel closer to difficult patients, helped them to cope in the ward. The type of music was unspecified, and in fact it appeared likely that in many instances it consisted mainly of radio and recorded music. (See rating of

3 & 4 above). Results were not significant, and this is probably because:

- there is no regular programme in music therapy in any of the establishments included.
- the establishments vary greatly in the extent to which music is used, depending on interests and skills of nursing staff.
- insufficient information was given in the questionnaire as to what e.g. "Music in the ward" actually implied.

Nevertheless, the individual answers (some of which included personal comments) indicated a general enthusiasm for having more music available, together with recognition of the difficulties for nurses who have no special skills in music. An exception was a nurse who wrote that she disliked having music in the ward because it built up an association in her mind between music and work-related stress, and that this carried over into her private life, thereby spoiling her personal enjoyment of music.

Because of the relatively small number of nurses who reported practical skills in playing a musical instrument - a total of only 27, of whom several noted "VERY Badly!" - it is clear that the responses represent fairly accurately the general state of musical activities, i.e. mainly recordings and radio music. One assumes that the employment of a professional music therapist as a visiting specialist or a permanent staff member would change this situation markedly.

How Can Music Therapy Reduce Staff Stress?

It is interesting to consider how many of the stress-producing behaviours listed in Section A would be reduced or even temporarily eliminated by a full program of music therapy. Music therapists are trained to work in dementia, and their training covers not only knowledge and understanding of the organic basis for dementia and difficult behaviour generally, but also the psychosocial aspects of emotional and psychiatric illness in the elderly. These include the prevalence of unresolved griefs and anger in the aged, including persons with advanced dementia. They also learn appropriate techniques for displacing anger and restlessness through appropriate music techniques, and so on. The use of music in counselling, for the amelioration of depressive and other illness, has long been advocated by the present author[7,8,9,10].

For full effectiveness there must be provision for group and individual work in music therapy. The group "singalong" or percussion band session does have merit, but, if this is all we do, we fail to meet the needs of the withdrawn and isolated, the sad and the depressed (the two are by no means synonymous), or the very special needs of those with aphasia in varying degrees of severity, those with impairment of body image and perceptual problems in general, the individual needs of the dying, the visually and/or hearing-impaired clients, the person with neurological disease or impairment (such as "stroke"), the older developmentally-delayed client, and so on. All of these problems may be met in those who also have organic brain dysfunction, and, even without such damage, those with the difficulties listed above can be "difficult", if their psychosocial needs are not met.

In practical terms it is heartening to staff, whether professional music therapists or not, to observe how aggressive behaviours diminish with the use of music as a therapeutic medium. One can assume that wandering is one factor in causing aggression between residents, because the wanderer is likely to tread on his neigbour's feet or otherwise bump into him, to interfere with his belongings, or - because of delusions and mistaken identity - one sees accusations and confrontation between people on matters which are not actually of any truth or relevance.

Restlessness may also be linked with aggression in that loss of purposeful activity may well lead to frustration and frustration to aggressive behaviour, so that to provide an activity in which success is possible, in a well-planned music therapy group, diminishes frustration and aggressive behaviours. Nurses say that boredom and inactivity are sure causes of aggressive behaviour, whether we are looking at young people in a confined space, or demented persons in the restricted area of a ward.

---

[7] Bright R. *Music in geriatric care*, (US Edition Musicgraphics, 1980) p.73.
[8] Bright R. *Practical planning in music therapy for the aged.* Alfred International, USA, 1984 p 33 onwards.
[9] Bright R. "Music and the management of grief reactions". (ed. Burnside) *Nursing and the Aged*, McGraw-Hill, USA, p 141 onwards.
[10] Bright R. *Grieving*, 1986. M.M.B. St Louis, USA.

I am grateful to Helen Odell, a music therapist working with psychogeriatric patients at Fulbourne Hospital, Cambridge, UK, for her careful observations of the extent to which there is generalisation of improved behaviour from the music therapy group to the ward. Her observations and those of nursing staff suggest that there is for a significant number of patients a decrease in aggressive behaviour for a time following the music group[11].

Music also gives to the demented person a feeling of enjoyment and well-being, a sense of normality, as well as making use of the residual powers of concentration in a planned activity, so that the sufferer is less likely to be irritated by other people.

Its orientating influence may also have an effect in reducing aggression because it is treating the person as an individual with some opportunity for free choice, affirming his existence as a person, and encouraging him to participate in an interesting activity. (See Chapter 5.)

The precise reasons for music's effects on demented persons are probably of trivial importance compared with the actual observed outcome, which is one of increased tranquillity and positive pleasure, not the pseudo-tranquillity of drug-induced immobility. Through music activities, planned with therapeutic goals in mind, we are giving to our demented patients an unique opportunity to be themselves!

---

[11]Odell H. Fulbourne Hospital, Cambridge, U.K., Personal Communication, 1985. re. Research Project, as yet unpublished.

CHAPTER 4

HOW MUSIC THERAPY HELPS DEMENTING PERSONS - II

Social Awareness and Communication

Although there are many musical pleasures which are enjoyed in solitude (such as the composition of music, the playing of solo works, the study of scores, reading about the lives and works of composers), music has also many social connotations, so that even the playing of solo works may be more enjoyable if we play to an enthusiastic audience (even if only one person), and we may gain more pleasure from listening to music when we listen in company with a friend or form part of an audience at a "live" concert.

For work with persons suffering from moderate or advanced dementia it is generally more satisfactory to work in the ward rather than taking patients to a separate music room. The advantages of ward work are firstly that the group members are in their familiar surroundings, so are likely to be more relaxed and less muddled, and secondly because there will be nursing staff available to help with toileting for those who have problems with continence.

The precise size of the therapeutic group is important; as a rough guide we may say that the more demented the persons, the smaller the group must be. For an extremely deteriorated person, work should be done initially at a one-to-one level, possibly drawing in one other person seated nearby so as to extend the stimulation and encourage somewhat wider social relationships than are possible for a dyad only.

Groups should never be more than ten, and even this number pre-supposes that there will be one or two helpers available so that the ratio of patients to staff is maintained at 3 or 4 to 1. If one has to work alone, it is more effective to spend five minutes with ten individuals in turn than to try to run a group for an hour with all ten people at once.

The seating plan is crucial to the outcome of our group work. NEVER put people in rows but in a small circle. The only exception to the need for a circle arrangement would be in a situation where no group work is planned but only individual interactions, in which case the seating plan is on the whole immaterial - although it is still true that people may gain stimulation from seeing other people joining in a music activity and be more inclined to participate when their turn comes.

The circle should be small enough to permit people to reach out and touch one another, but not so close that elbows jog each other, and there is a sense of overcrowding - since this is inimical to good relationships, and has been found to have an adverse effect upon patients in institutions[1].

To have a small circle permits each participant to see and hear what is happening in the other parts of the group. Visual and hearing losses are common in older people, and, when concentration is compromised anyway, we must do our best to ensure that conditions are at their best for maximum awareness of what is going on in the activity.

Singing together - formally in a choir or informally in a singalong - is one such shared pleasure, and many people have happy memories of occasions throughout the life-span when singing together was enjoyed. Singing a college song, the national anthem, a hymn or Sunday school song, songs shared in courtship, singing at a picnic or cook-out (barbecue) - these and many other happenings live on in our memories as occasions in which the event is permanently linked with the singing we shared.

It is fortunate that, even for the person with moderately advanced dementia, singing is still enjoyable, so long as the music is chosen with empathy and knowledge of the person's needs, and so long as we can accept the need for informality of atmosphere.

One generally assumes that the music will be from the past, and certainly if it is impossible to find out from the person concerned what his favourites are, and the family is unavailable to give information on this, then the safest choice is music popular at the time the person was in their early adult life.

---

[1]Boucher M.L. "Personal space and chronicity in the mental hospital. *Perspectives psychiat. care*, Sept/Oct 1971, **9**, pp 206-210.

For example, for a person aged 86 in 1988, one would select first of all music which was popular in the years 1919 - 1928, more or less. There is no precise cut-off point because in some families parents and grandparents sang and played music, so that the children grew up with a familiarity with music from previous generations, and these memories remain into old age and even in dementia. One would try to give a selection of the then-equivalent of Pop music, also music of the sentimental ballad type, as well as the "serious" music which is of a more timeless quality, and which gives pleasure either in listening or encouraging the person to hum the melodies as they are played. Works suitable for this would include Chopin, some of Tchaikowsky, Mendelssohn, Grieg as being the easy-listening variety of classical music.

Responses to these offerings of different types of music (spread over a few sessions, not poured out all at one sitting!) will give a clear indication as to where to go next in choosing music for listening.

Knowing that the demented person used to sing in a choir, attend ballet performances, operas, or symphony concerts, was a composer in a minor degree - all these and other clues will help us plan programmes with the best possible therapeutic outcome, dealing with responses as they arise.

If one knows even a little of their social and educational background, then this too provides a clue to help choose the right type of music, e.g., if the person has been an enthusiastic player of the home organ, with a known repertoire of favourites, then this suggests one direction for music, even though there may be some sadness that the skills are largely lost, and here we must give the utmost in empathy even if the words we use are not totally understood.

(See Chapter 7 for comments on involving and helping the family.)

Group singalongs can also be used therapeutically to enhance awareness of other people and of the environment. The programmes should be planned in advance so that the introductory part of the session consists of music which is known to be familiar to the people in the group, in order to set up a cheerful atmosphere of participation.

We may achieve stimulation of cognitive activity and social relationships by passing something around the circle from hand to hand. We should note that although it is far easier to show a picture than to pass a real thing around the circle, the picture is an unsatisfactory substitute for the look and feel of the genuine object.

There is no comparison in the stimulus of even a good photograph compared with the reality of, say, an old straw hat passed around from hand to hand, when one can feel the texture of the straw, try it on for size perhaps and share a smile at the appearance, with all the memories evoked either of Shirley Temple singing the song of that name, or of oneself wearing an old straw hat around the garden or farm.

The object chosen should be such that a song is linked with it, and it is perhaps surprising to observe the manner in which people suffering from dementia do have their memories jogged by having something in their hand which suggests a song title or words. We note also the social contact which is elicited as the passing around is in progress.

A teddy bear, for example, produces an immediate response "*The Teddy Bear's Picnic*," either spoken or sung by one or more members of the group, and to pass the soft, furry toy around elicits caring and nurturing responses from many of the most deteriorated people present.

A rose passed around will elicit many ideas for songs such as *Rose of Tralee*, *Sweet Rosie O'Grady*, *Roses of Picardy* and so on. A packet of tea will remind people of the song *Tea for Two*, etc. This is not basically any different from work in an everyday geriatric group, but the objects to be used must be selected with more care to ensure that the linked songs will be known by the members of the group.

In such work, we are providing cues to enhance the remembering process, and we have noted that retrieval from long-term memory in demented subjects is assisted by the giving of cues[2]. One of the advantages of this type of group work is that the tactile sense, the visual sense and the olfactory sense may all be

---

[2]Morris R. et al "Retrieval from long-term memory in senile dementia. Cued recall revisited." *Brit. Jnl. clin. psychol.* 1983, 22, pp 141-142.

stimulated, and in dementia it is vital that we approach people by several sensory pathways for maximum effect, although without producing confusion. Thus one passes around only one object at a time.

More important, the passing around of such items may elicit not only musical memories but also reminiscence and social interaction. This must be facilitated by the group leader, and may initially meet with little response, but perseverance usually gains a measure of success.

"Success" in work for dementing clients is measured more modestly than with an ordinary geriatric group, but is nonetheless significant. If one notes a lifting of depression during a music session, or if one observes an exchange of smiles from one person to another as a flower is passed around the circle, then one can justifiably enjoy a sense of success, which reflects the success experienced by the client.

Following this introductory section, one can build on the awareness which passing objects around and singing together has produced in order to give formal introductions between neighbours in the group. One can use songs which mention names, such as "Mary", "Jean", "Frankie & Johnnie" as a help to such introductions. Some people may prefer to use name introductions first, but the author finds that, in dementia programmes, there are some advantages in bringing the group to some degree of concentration by a definite activity first, before starting the more intimate procedure of introducing people to each other.

There is a dilemma as to whether one should use first names or formal titles of "Mr" , "Mrs" and so on. Some elderly ladies have forgotten their married names and are more likely to respond to their first names, and some still-verbal people have expressed a preference for using first names as being friendlier and making them feel more at home. Since "feeling at home" in an institution is one of our prime aims, the use of "Mary", "Bob" etc is for most people justified for that reason. We must note, nevertheless that there are those who firmly wish to be addressed formally as "Mr", "Mrs", Miss", and there are also those members of staff who are uncomfortable using first names. In both instances, formality is essential.

One can point out the colours of clothes which people are wearing and play tunes or songs which mention those colours - *The Blue Danube, Alice Blue Gown* for blue, *The Red Red Robin* or *Red Sails in the Sunset* for red, *Greensleeves* for green and so on. All these and many other techniques, which the imaginative and innovative therapist will devise, increase awareness of other people.

Being aware of one's environment raises some problems, in that "Reality Orientation" has become almost a "dirty word" for some of us, with its routine questions asked over and over again, with little understanding of how it must feel to be asked every day questions to which you do not know the answers.

The rationalisation seems to be that if people have forgotten anyway, then the constant repetition is not harmful, and that if you ask the same questions about time, place etc every day they may eventually remember the answer.

But it seems likely that people do remember the sense of being under pressure and the awareness of failure, even if they do not recall the precise nature of the question and answer, so that we must devise more positive approaches to Reality Orientation.

Far more empathic and productive is the affirmative approach, in which one gives people the information they need, saying, for example "Good morning, Mr Smith, I'm the social worker. Isn't it a cold day, considering we are in the middle of Summer? We don't often get a day as cold as this in August/February (depending on which hemisphere you live in!)." Or, alternatively, "Isn't it a lovely Summer's day - just right for the month of ....!"

A Sydney Social Worker, Barbara Squires, who was involved in the development of this approach, says she always knows that the approach is winning when a demented resident of the nursing home greets her with a mischievous smile and says, "Hullo, you're Barbara Squires, the social worker, and it's Wednesday today!"

Another area of information: "It's Thursday today, and we always have music in the upstairs sitting room on Thursdays, just after morning coffee break. I do hope you will be able to join us up there, we always enjoy your singing of ....." or "It's Saturday today, and your daughter will be coming to visit you after lunch - you remember that she has moved to a house quite near here, in ...., so that it is easy for her to come and see you each Saturday afternoon." "Perhaps your daughter will bring her children with her, your grandchildren Peter and Caroline, now that they are 7 and 9 they can walk all the way here!"

These and similar approaches are a far more empathic way of giving orientation in time and place and person than the constant questioning so popular in times past. As several geriatricians have said "Is knowing the day of the week really such an important accomplishment for an elderly person in hospital? And how many of us, when on holiday with nothing much to mark the different days of the week, find ourselves incapable of saying instantly whether it is Tuesday or Wednesday?!"

What IS important is that the dementing person retains an awareness of the place in which they live, of those who love them and care for them, those with whom they share a home - and "to heck with" *formal* questions about date and weather, as an activity unrelated to affectionate relationships. To use music to support this affirmative reality orientation is a happy way of achieving this awareness. No ground-rules can be given, but the innovative therapist will evolve techniques which are constantly renewed in a creative way, not simply a matter of learning a sure-fire technique and flipping the switch to put it into practice mechanically, day after day!

It is easy to see how music can be incorporated into this empathic approach to Reality Orientation: there are many songs which mention the weather, and they can be chosen by someone in the group after everyone has looked out of the window to decide what kind of day it is outside. Seasons of the year can be reinforced by songs such as "Autumn Leaves", either on record or sung by the therapist and/or the group, together with a beautiful spray of red and gold leaves to remind people of the beauty of Fall. And so on.

Most music therapists and other helpers like to use musical instruments as part of a programme. The author has mixed feelings about these, because of observations of sessions in which instruments have been used without proper empathic introduction. If people are afraid that they are "in their second childhood" (a common fear as the memory starts to deteriorate, when the sufferer is aware of his own disintegration), to have a small tambourine thrust into the hand without any supportive explanation can reinforce one's worst fears.

But if we present the activity with loving care, the playing of musical instruments can be most enjoyable, adding to the feelings of success for those who are otherwise almost entirely bereft of this satisfying emotion.

General principles which the author follows are:

- Don't have instruments every time; retain a certain sense of novelty. Although it is improbable that patients will recall plans made at the previous session, one can at least mention that a decision had been made the week before to bring the boxes of instruments.

- Don't have enough to go round; this means that the unwilling person can pass the instrument on to someone else, and - with luck - one may even establish a kind of (benevolent) competitive desire to "have a go," so that the instruments become sought-after rather than rejected.

  Or, alternatively, have the box of instruments on the floor in the middle of the room so that those who wish can help themselves from the supply without any compulsion, as well as having the pleasure of making a decision as to which instrument each person wants to play.

- Be sure to have instruments of good quality, not trashy, tinny bits of painted metal. Good instruments are costly, but their purchase says something, even to a demented person, about how we value him. (This is not only true of musical instruments but also about the clothes we dress people in, the food we give them to eat and the way we serve it, the way we speak to them - using their names or just saying, "Come on, Pop!")

Instruments can be used to back up singing or as a separate activity, or both. But one should not either encourage or permit the endless thumping which in some places passes for music therapy, as a constant background to all singing and all conversation.

There should be a definite starting point and a finishing point, so that participants are encouraged to concentrate on what is taking place. It may be appropriate to have a conductor, someone who enjoys wielding a baton, but with a group of persons with advanced dementia it will probably not be possible for a patient to do this.

In our planning, we must not forget that there are various factors limiting the awareness of which people are capable. We have already mentioned many of them - visual defects, deafness, cognitive losses which give the effect of living life in horse-blinkers, a kind of cognitive tunnel vision.

There are also the neurological deficits such as loss of visual fields in hemianopia, neglect of one side of the total environment due to brain damage. Relationships are also hampered by difficulty in language processing (dysphasia) as the result of stroke or other brain damage, so that one cannot put thoughts into words, and possibly cannot even think in any normal manner. Or there are difficulties in actual pronunciation (dysarthria), as in multiple sclerosis, when the vocal musculature is weak and inadequate, or in Parkinson's disease, when the voice is weak and lacks normal inflexions, or in Huntington's disease, in which there is inadequate control over musculature with spasms affecting speech as well as all other activities.

All these impairments reduce one's capacity for social awareness and relationships, and when they are added to advanced dementing processes, the difficulties are unimaginable.

In working with persons who are aphasic as the result of brain damage, whether or not this is also linked to the dementia syndrome, it will be noted that even if unable to speak, the person can often sing, to the extent sometimes of singing the words correctly. There may be little or no comprehension of the meaning of the words, it may be an automatic response, but this is unimportant; the main aim is to give to the sufferer an opportunity for success and enjoyment. Although some speech pathologist, use melodic intonation therapy[3] in order to enhance propositional speech in stroke patients, such programmes would be inappropriate for dementing persons and should not be attempted because of the probability (amounting to a certainty) of causing frustration and emotional suffering because of the impossible demands which would be made by such a therapeutic regime.

Encouraging our clients to look at each other, to smile, to touch or hold hands — these basic social interactions are all facilitated by our music sessions. They have enormous value in keeping alive or rekindling a sense of belonging, being loved and quite literally of being in touch with each other, even when speech and general cognition have almost disappeared.

Despite the difficulties and limitations imposed by the dementing process, we can hope that, through music programmes, we shall be able to bring some enjoyment of social relationships and achievement, thereby improving the quality of life.

---

[3]Albert M. et al "Melodic intonation therapy for aphasia." *Arch. neurol.*, 1973, 29 (2), pp 130-131

CHAPTER 5

HOW MUSIC THERAPY HELPS DEMENTING PERSONS - III

Mobilisation

Why mobilise people anyway? So many of them fall over that isn't it easier to keep them tied down in chairs?

It is an unfortunate fact that in some places for the aged restraints are used consistently, and sometimes this is done to protect the establishment from prosecution by relatives if a wandering demented person has a fall. However, their use is counter-productive, because those who are constantly tied down suffer from constant frustration and anger, and become harder rather than easier to manage, and when they do eventually get loose from their chair-prison, they are likely to have muscles weakened by inactivity, even to the extent of having developed contractures, and are more likely to have falls because of their enforced immobility.

It is recognised that there may be occasions with wanderers when restraint is needed as a temporary measure only, for not more than a brief space of time, and also that there are methods of discouraging people from constantly moving about which are not objectionable, so long as they are used for only a small part of each day. Such methods include the use of "bean-bag chairs", in which the person is close to the ground so that he cannot fall far, but it is hard to get up out of the chair, so that constant wandering and aggression is prevented. These chairs have the advantage that, since they are filled with small beads of foam plastic, they have no hard edges so that it is improbable that circulation will be impeded or that pressure areas occur, but they permit considerable freedom of movement whilst at the same time reducing wandering.

Another device is the chair which has a table across the front. This is acceptable, so long as it is used to make life interesting by providing an activity on its surface (even if this activity is only the constant folding, unfolding and refolding table napkins!), and the table is not used merely as a barrier.

But, in the opinion of the author and many others who are involved in the care of the dementing population, such devices should be a last resort, used for short periods and not to be regarded as a complete management approach.

In New York in 1985, at the International Congress on Gerontology, a research project in Canada was described[1]. In this project, records were kept of the use of restraints and the use of psychotropic tranquillising drugs. Hospital staff foretold a disastrous outcome, saying that if people were not restrained, there would be :

- injuries and
- an increased need for tranquillisers to keep people at peace with one another.

As a start to the programme, relatives were given an explanation of why it was important to give their dementing people freedom even if it meant a slightly increased risk of falls, and relatives were all asked to sign a release, absolving the establishment from legal liability if the new-found freedom did lead to a fracture or other injury. With that dealt with, staff became happier with the project, and it was found after the passage of many months that, far from causing an increase in the use of tranquillisers, the cessation of the use of restraints led to a reduced demand for sedation. Although there was a slight increase in the number of falls, there was no increase in the number of injuries requiring treatment which resulted from those falls.

The conclusion was clear - people are angrier and harder to manage when they are tied to a chair than when they are free to move around. Lists of injuries suggested that there is no great rise in numbers of fractured femurs or other major hurts as a consequence of the gift of freedom to move, and that the freedom to move is of far greater importance than the possible dangers of the demented elderly person's falling.

We must be aware of the guilty feelings experienced by many relatives who have eventually placed their dementing person in an institution, and of the anger they experience with the institution if any harm befalls

---

[1]Powell C. et al "Freedom from restraint. Consequences of reducing physical restraints in treatment of elderly people. Abstracts of 1985 International Congress on Gerontology, New York.

the person concerned. This anger is the way in which those with guilty feelings cope with this guilt; it is seen not only in relatives of dementing persons but in, for example, parents of developmentally-disabled children if those children have to be placed in institutional care for one reason or another. Parents readily feel angry if there is a mishap or if they feel that the care given by the institution is not equal to the care the person previously received at home.

It would seem that much of the defensiveness observed in staff of institutions about possible falls, and their continuing use of restraints to prevent such falls, results from fear of the anger of relatives, and of litigation if there is a mishap.

One must assume that if better counselling were given to relatives at the time of admission to institutional care, there would be less guilt, less demand for restraints, and less anger with the establishments if restraints are not used, even allowing for the risks of falls. The end result of this counselling would be more tranquillity for the dementing persons in being given more freedom and being allowed to take minor risks!

In planning work in music for mobility, we must not forget the many limiting factors seen in persons who are dementing, limitations which may be imposed by their fundamental dementing process or which are caused by another condition. Some mention of these has already been made in the preceding chapter, but we must think about them again in considering mobility work for dementing persons who are in an advanced stage of the process.

Because of memory failure there will be difficulties in carrying out any sequence of actions, and even the simplest instruction, "Stamp one foot and then the other" may be beyond the grasp and memory of persons with advanced dementia.

As has already been noted (see Chapter 1), dementia of the Alzheimer type frequently affects the parietal lobes, so that it is difficult or totally impossible for the dementing sufferer to conceptualise any movements demonstrated to him by a therapist and to put these into effect in his own limbs and trunk.

Because of difficulties in sequences and in body image, it is best that exercises should be limited to movements which come more or less naturally - keeping time with the music by marking time on the floor; clapping in time to the music; rocking to and fro in time with a gentle swaying tune; joining hands around the circle and moving from side to side with a well-known waltz; rising to one's feet to do a simple dance. Depending on the level of one's functioning this will more or less resemble dances we performed in the past. Or we may lead people in marching around the room hand in hand as a stirring march is played.

These and other activities need little or no explanation, so that even non-verbal people can join in the activity. Nor do the movements need accurate body image to achieve performance, so that those with visual field losses or neglect can often participate to their own satisfaction.

Marching around the room hand in hand as the music plays is a particularly useful activity, it seems to re-activate old memory traces of games played as children, and - whilst in no way treating people as if they are childish - enables them to function to their own satisfaction by this shared activity. The precise method consists of the therapist or co-therapist reaching out a hand towards a seated client, encouraging that person to take the hand of another person, and so on, until possibly the whole group is up, walking or marching around the room in a long line. From this, one may be able to lead into a follow-the-leader activity, or a Conga dance. Even though the extent of actions will be severely limited by frailty or inability to comprehend precisely what is going on, it will be FUN!

Mobility For Those in Early Stages of Dementia

(There is an overlap here between movement as such and creativity. See the chapter which follows.)

What can be planned will depend on the level of functioning of the clients in the group. For some groups, who (because they are in the very early stages of the dementing process) are likely to be in community day-care programmes rather than full-time institutional care, the author has found that very simple folk dances are enjoyed and are performed quite well. These can be walked at a moderate pace; there is no need to run or skip, as younger persons would wish to do.

Dance 1. High level of functioning

For groups of six or eight persons. For the sequence given below, the British dance ***The Sailors' Hornpipe*** or the USA song *Polly-wolly Doodle* would be suitable, or any music of strong rhythmic pattern consisting of 4-bar (4-measure) phrases and a total length which is a multiple of 16 bars (measures). e.g. many Scottish country dances.

Use music as suggested above, with a 4/4 beat at about the rate M.M.120 to give ample time for walking the steps of the dance. But note that the dance is walked at the rate of only TWO steps per measure, i.e. one step per minim (half note) so that the actual steps (or claps, in phase 2) are at the rate of 60 per minute. This can be speeded up, the accompanist playing a little faster (the author uses a piano accordion so as to be close to the action), so that - if members can become more proficient and brisker in their movements - the dance may eventually be done with a lively recorded accompaniment.

Preparation:
Place all the couples in two lines facing each other, leaving a gap of about two metres (six feet) between the two lines, to give space for dancing between the lines.
Clapping can continue throughout the dance so that everyone is doing something all the time, while watching the dancers.

Phase 1. The top couple moves to the centre for 4 bars, i.e. 8 steps forward, until they stand close together facing one another.

Phase 2. They then clap alternately their own hands and their partner's hands, repeated 4 times, a total of 8 claps.

Phase 3. They then join hands and circle clockwise for 8 counts.

Phase 4. Still holding hands, the top couple then moves down the line for 8 bars of music, until they drop hands as they take their places at the bottom end of the two lines while the others move up to keep the double line more or less in the same area of the room.

The sequence is then repeated with the new couple at the top of the lines.

If wished, everyone can do the steps together, with extra circling in the opposite direction to fill the time which is otherwise taken by the top couple moving down the line.

Dance 2. For people with a lower level of functioning

This can be done by any number of people between 6 and 12.

The Merry Widow Waltz by Lehar or any Viennese waltz can be used, played briskly, at a speed of one bar (measure) = MM 60.
(It is best not to use recorded music because recorded concert versions of waltzes usually have marked rubato so that steady steps are impossible.)

The movements as set out below take up therefore a total of 32 bars (measures), and most waltzes have a pattern in multiples of 16 or of 32 measures.

Preparation: Stand people in a circle holding hands all around the group.
1. Holding hands, move into the centre of the circle for 4 steps.
2. Holding hands, back again as before for 4 counts.
3. Repeat 1., moving into centre.
4. Repeat 2., moving back.
5. Drop hands and clap 8 times. (If it is considered that dropping and re-joining hands is too complex, the stamping the feet can be substituted for the clapping, or the dance can consist only of steps 1-4 above.)

6. Re-join hands and everyone moves together around the circle for 8 counts.

Similar quasi-folk dances will be constructed by the imaginative therapist to suit the capabilities of the individuals and groups involved. Dances involving the circle with all clients holding hands give better sense of involvement and require less comprehension of instructions and sequences. They also have the advantage of providing support for those with compromised sense of balance. Furthermore, as everyone is involved simultaneously, there is no problem of loss of concentration from the group whilst one couple carries out a particular routine of movements.

Creativity involves the therapist as well as the client!

Sailor's Hornpipe, steps marked with numbers:

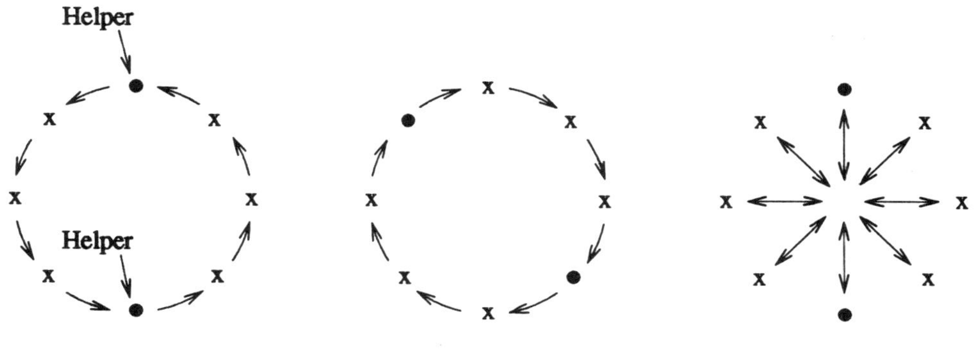

1. 8 steps anticlockwise   2. 8 steps clockwise   3. To centre and back, 4 steps each

Clapping games from childhood can also be used, depending on the traditional activities known to members of the group. It can be stimulating for the group to watch a younger person (e.g. a visiting child or a young therapist), skipping with a rope whilst skipping rhymes are recited, encouraging the onlookers to clap in time, and perhaps to recite the rhymes they can recall.

The exact choice of folk dances, clapping games, skipping rhymes, and so on must be determined on the basis of familiarity, but if there is one person in the group who has clear memories of an ethnic dance, then it will not harm the others in the group to try it, so long as it remains enjoyable and not a revelation of incompetence and failure.

If necessary, the creative therapist will (as noted above) be able to invent suitable dances which make few demands upon the failing memory for sequences, the failing body-image and the failing concentration, and which concentrate instead upon simple movements in which a staff member can work hand in hand with a patient to achieve the maximum in fun and sense of achievement.

Such activities can help the observant therapist to assist in differential diagnosis between true dementia and pseudo-dementia/late-onset psychiatric illness. It is rare for a person who can follow directions and sequences to be a "genuine" dementia sufferer; it is more likely that the apparent dementing condition is really a psychiatric illness. Such observations will help other members of the clinical team in planning the best treatment approach.

The aim of any total mobility programme should be to provide opportunities for moving all body joints and systems, but within the limits of pain and without risking exacerbating cardiac problems or respiratory insufficiency. Many elderly people suffer from balance problems or generalised giddiness, so that one should avoid brisk or extensive head movements because of the risks of vertigo.

A suitable maintenance programme includes:

1. Shoulder "wiggling" in time to jazz music; this also helps to keep the spine mobile.
2. Side-to-side movements to emphasise body symmetry by folding the arms and rocking from side to side in time to music such as the Scots tune *The Skye Boat Song* or a slow waltz.
3. Exercise of the quadriceps muscles (the strong muscles above the knee which are essential to walking and preventing knee damage) by marching on the spot, even if only whilst seated, and doing the *Can-Can* by upward kicks whilst seated.
4. Finger dexterity can be maintained by encouraging people to "play the piano" whilst the therapist plays rapid pieces of music which encourage finger work.
5. Ankle mobility by circling the toe to match a waltz tune, so that the toe moves through a wide circle.
6. Supination/pronation of the arm is achieved by extending the arms in front, with the palms alternately facing up and down, to a brisk march tune.
7. Ventilation of the lungs is encouraged by taking a few (two or three) deep breaths and having a good cough. If this is not understood, the aim may be achieved by suggesting that "we'll see how long we can sing without taking a breath", but this must be done only once, to avoid hyper-ventilation and giddiness.
8. Balance is frequently impaired in extreme old age and/or in dementia, so that it is helpful to have the whole group standing in a circle holding hands (with nurses/aides assisting) and - to the accompaniment of a slow waltz such as *The Merry Widow* - swing each foot in turn across the mid-line.
9. Sometimes one or two people will rise to their feet and dance, reaching out to someone else as a partner, and such spontaneous activity is to be encouraged, even if the dancing is of a very simple nature.

One demented Polish gentleman who showed no response to any aspect of the ward programme, and who sat constantly with his forearms on his knees, head bowed and hat pulled well down over his eyes, stood up straight, smiled and danced traditional Polish folk dances when Polish dance tunes were played. He stamped his feet, slapped his thighs, swung around from side to side swinging his arms wide between the thigh-slapping, and smiled, at the same time inviting by gesture the physiotherapist to dance with him.

Another woman (whose customary attitude is to lie curled up in a foetal posture on the floor), claps with the music, copies some of the movements as far as she is able, and looks a different person while the music continues. Unfortunately this is only a short-lived improvement, but it is not for that reason to be regarded as worthless.

A man with dementia resulting from normal-pressure hydrocephalus, who - before his shunt was inserted - lived in a state of constant bewilderment, was yet able to sing the words of all the songs appropriate to his age, and looked happy as long as the music was in progress, tapping his feet in time with the music although he was incapable of carrying out any instructions related to movements.

If we know that a patient has such a shunt and one then notices sudden changes in behaviour in music and movement sessions, especially changes of alertness, continence and balance, one should pass on such observations to other clinical staff, since the changes may well indicate that the shunt has blocked.

Summary

As long as we recognise and allow for the various disabilities of our dementing clients, a mobilisation programme allied with appropriate music brings to the individual and to the group some sense of well-being and may help to use constructively some of the energy which otherwise keeps restless patients on the go the whole time. Music must be chosen from that which is likely to be familiar to the members of the group, and, for preference, should be played on a firm-toned portable instrument such as the piano accordion, which can be played on the move and which helps people to feel in touch with what is going on.

The Dying Patient

The special needs in work with a dying dementing person will depend on the level of the person's cognitive functioning at the time.

For example, a person who is dying from cancer during the early stages of the dementing process will have considerable awareness of what is happening, even if the level of comprehension fluctuates somewhat, and may be able to realise when the end is approaching. On the other hand, a person who is dying after many years of increasing deterioration may have little real comprehension of what is going on, and it may be extremely difficult to decide what needs to be said or done.

The music therapist is at a great advantage in that the relationships can be basically non-verbal, and one can observe responses to the music which is played at the bedside to assess what one does or says next.

The person who is able to understand the implications of the illness and the treatment regime will need the same empathy as the non-dementing person, the same opportunity for tying off loose ends of relationships with the family and friends, the same chance to say farewell. When the patient is well able to communicate with us, we can play the pieces of music which he or she has requested with some expectation that the patient's choice will lead on to the level of conversation which he needs.

As with all our work in therapy and counselling with those who are dying, we do not impose our own stereotypes of attitudes to death[2]. There may be a deep need for denial or the patient's memory status and loss of insight may make it impossible for him to realise that death is approaching[3].

Sometimes one finds that the dying person says something to this effect: "O well, never mind, I will be better next week when you come to see me; this is just a temporary set-back." If the person is in fact having increasingly frequent pain medication, increasing weakness and loss of weight, all of which would tell a non-demented person that he was gravely ill, then there is no point in trying to lead the conversation further; all we can do is provide distraction from pain and a temporary pleasant break from hospital routine.

If, however, the person takes up our cue of, say, religious music or music from his own life history to comment at length on looking back over life, and if he speaks openly about life after death and of his own belief or lack of belief in survival of the soul, then we can know that he is probably aware of impending death and we can follow up his lead in whichever direction he takes us.

With the extremely deteriorated individual, we have no way of telling what thought processes are possible, and it is the author's practice to speak to the person as if he could understand what is being said, but without any words which could be frightening.

"I am playing this hymn because your daughter tells me you used to sing it in the Church choir. You may find it will comfort you at this time when you are having so much pain."

---

[2]Bright R. Grieving. op. cit. page 56
[3]Op cit page 55.

"I am sorry you are having a difficult time with pain and lots of injections, it must be rather frightening for you but there will always be someone with you when you need help and comfort. I'll play so-and-so for you, I know you always used to ask for that piece and perhaps it will help a bit!"

The promise that the person will not be left alone must not, of course, be made if there is any doubt about this, but most units for the care of the dying do make a firm commitment that no one will die alone.

The family of the dementing person will need a great deal of support at this time, because of the probability of ambivalent feelings about the impending death. On the one hand there will be feelings of relief that the end is near - the end not only of the suffering of the patient but of the strain which the dementia has placed on their own lives.

On the other hand there will be sadness at the way things have happened, the sadness from observing the increasing mental deterioration of the loved person, and probably some feelings of guilt that they had not done more, visited more often, or been more patient. (These guilty feelings are commonly experienced even by the most loving and supportive of relatives.)

Through our music intervention at the bedside we may be able to help the family to feel that they are involved in those last days of care (thereby lessening their guilty feelings) and help them to cope with the separation. No instructions or advice can be given - all depends upon the way the therapeutic relationship develops - but we can have some hope of assisting the family even if it may appear that we are doing little for the dying demented person.

The care of the dying is always a challenge to our empathy and to our own thinking about life and death, and work with the dying person who is also dementing provides us with a double challenge. Through the empathic use of music, it may be possible to meet those challenges and give to both patient and family a sense of being understood and comforted in a way which is otherwise unavailable.

CHAPTER 6

CREATIVITY FOR THE DEMENTING CLIENT

"Can persons with dementia really be creative? Isn't all their cognitive function too deteriorated to permit creative activity?"

The implication of these queries is probably based fairly soundly on fact if we are looking at the person with advanced dementia and think of creativity as being entirely cognitive in origin, or if our ideas of what constitutes "creativity" are over- ambitious, based perhaps on creativity in intact young adults.

But does creativity necessarily involve high-level cognitive functioning? Can we have less ambitious ways of looking at creativity?

The way one defines "creativity" is largely personal, but to the author it includes exploration - of oneself, of one's surroundings and one's relationships; newness, even if this consists only of rediscovery of forgotten joys; the ability to be oneself and follow one's own star, with active involvement.

There will be those who will laugh at such ideas as applied to those with dementia, but is it all so impossible? Cannot even dementing persons, in the early stages of the disease or further along the line, follow up something which is personal? Rediscover some old enjoyment, perhaps in a new way? Explore the possibilities of musical instruments which were previously unfamiliar? Levels of achievement will be severely restricted and it is no kindness to a dementing person to expect from her more than she can perform, but - from the joy which is seen on the faces of patients, even those who are unable to speak or communicate in any way - it is clear that there are satisfactions which cannot be described but which are none the less real.

By creativity we may mean something as simple as inventing a new way of jiggling one's hips to the music, playing an unfamiliar musical instrument, or singing louder or softer as indicated by a conductor. It may be that old skills are being used, but the general atmosphere achieved will be one of involvement, innovation and creativity.

In the chapter on mobility, we have seen how simple folk-dancing can be enjoyed by persons who are in early stages of dementia, when there is still retained an ability to follow a simple direction or a sequence of two or three movements, given assistance by staff. Moving to music enhances a feeling of creativity and enjoyment, even though the movements of the activity have been planned by the therapist in advance.

Even if we are doing simple "ballroom" dancing, in which old skills are being used (e.g. holding hands while we sway from side to side), there is still a genuine sharing of pleasure, a sense of exploration of space, a new way of using one's body, which is essentially creative, and which elicits responses far beyond what might be expected in the dementing client.

Movement with music may help to discharge some of the anxiety experienced by dementing clients. One notices the restlessness of many such people, not necessarily full-scale wandering but the restless behaviour which keeps body parts in constant minor motion. This is described by some observers as being needed to discharge anxiety, and - if this is indeed so - purposeful physical activity in creative movement may be still more effective, so long as one does not induce more anxiety by giving instructions - making demands - inducing a sense of right and wrong.

It is possible that, in this principle of using physical movement to discharge anxiety, we can draw an analogy with the "Running Treatment" of panic states, in which persons suffering from this problem find that the panic is reduced by strong physical effort[1].

Another helpful aspect of free creative movement is that it must necessarily take place in a large area of space, and to enjoy freedom of movement is a privilege often not available for the resident of a psychiatric hospital or nursing home. It has been noted in Chapter 4 that over-crowding contributes to chronicity in psychiatric wards, and, since demented persons are frequently cared for in psychogeriatric wards of large

---

[1]Orwin A — "The running treatment: a preliminary communication on a new use for an old therapy." *Brit. Jnl. Psychiat.* 1973, **122**, pp 175-179

institutions, the space and freedom to use that space in our movement-and-music sessions is likely to be of value.

In the book *Teaching Dance Skills to Senior Adults*[2] Lerman refers to and illustrates work in mime, in which emotions and abstract concepts are presented and expressed through movement. We must not expect that our dementing clients, with their characteristic difficulty in thinking in abstract concepts, will be able to do this, but we may, nevertheless, be able to work out some basic emotions through movement supported by appropriate music.

Chiffon scarves may prove to be helpful in promoting initiative in movement; care must be taken because persons with advanced dementing conditions may not have any idea how to use them but will suck them, tear them up, tie them in knots. Others will put them in their pockets or handbags (pocket-books), but this does not matter; the scarves can be retrieved unharmed.

Some people show hitherto unsuspected skills of grace and movement when given a scarf. One such lady moved from side to side to the rhythm of a tango, entirely confounding the matron of the nursing home who had said, regrettably in tones of scorn, "SHE'll never do anything!"

Mention has already been made of the tact required to present musical instruments of the simple percussion type, and this cannot be emphasised too strongly. It may be necessary to start with one person playing an instrument (in any group there is usually one person, even if it is a member of staff, who enjoys such participation) and hoping that the idea is "infectious" !

The author has on many occasions used an autoharp, in which the client simply holds a plectrum while the therapist manipulates the chord-bars. A rubber door-wedge makes a good plectrum because it is easy to hold, and produces a pleasant tone, it is also less likely than a hard-edged tool to jam under or against the strings. [For this suggestion I am grateful to Clive Robbins.] Even though the chords are made by the therapist, with someone else perhaps singing a melody, the client gains a sense of enjoyment in the participation, and this is in itself creative. It may also be possible to help the client to hold down the bars instead, whilst the therapist sweeps the plectrum, but it is unlikely that the demented client will be able to do both at once since the action of the right hand is so very different from that of the left, and we know that parietal dysfunction is common in dementia.

Bongo drums can be shared by two players, it may be necessary at first to have a patient share with a staff member, but one's aim would be to encourage two patients to share the pair of drums. At first the music is likely to be purely imitative, but, in the absence of piano or recorded accompaniment, it is possible for creative rhythmic work to begin, even though one tends to see perseveration - i.e. an idea repeated. This can happen with words or with actions, and is characteristic of certain cortical lesions[3].

A set of chime bars can be used to enhance exploration, which is to be regarded as an essential part of creativity; it is important that the beater chosen is the right type, there are few sounds which are more dead than the dull "thuck" of a beater on a chime bar when there is no bounce-off of the head. A fibreglass head seems to produce a bright ringing tone even in the hand of the inexpert, the hardness causes it to bounce off even without any intention on the part of the player.

Playing the set of chime bars should not be restricted to accompanying a given melody; although it is far harder to encourage improvisation than to follow a set pattern, the results - if it can be done - outweigh the effort. It will probably be necessary to demonstrate what can be done, e.g., sweeping the beater right up the whole set to produce a sliding scale up and then down, and again one may see perseveration and also echopraxia - the imitation of movements as an automatic response. But, once started, one may at least hope for something more than mere imitation, we may hope for a few changes to what is done. And if the outcome IS only imitation, it offers the possibility that some subtle enjoyment is achieved for the player and the listener.

---

[2]Lerman L. *Teaching dance skills to senior adults.* Charles Thomas, Springfield Ill, USA, 1984

[3]Mifka P. "Discussion of perseverance in post-traumatic psychiatric disturbances." *Vol 24 of Handbook of Clinical Neurology, ed. Vincken & Bruyn.* North Holland, 1977, pp 550-551.

One needs to be aware that to play an accompaniment or put on a tape/record of band music is often counter-productive in enhancing creativity, even though it does produce an instant result. If mechanically produced or even live music is played, then the incentive to "do one's own thing" evaporates and the percussion instruments are used simply as a rhythm band in a way which usually fails to develop creativity.

There are times when a rhythm band is appropriate, when the aim is "instant sound" (especially for an extremely deteriorated group of persons), but friendly silence, i.e., no formal accompaniment, but simply friendly encouragement, is more helpful if one's therapeutic goal is to enhance the creative spirit. When taking part in such a programme, it is encouraging to see how rapidly a group of demented persons begin to make their own sounds, even in the absence of background accompanying music, and the extent to which they appear to become aware of each other's playing.

The therapist may choose to play a single chime bar or some other non-overpowering instrument to encourage participation, and may eventually decide to take up the group's musically developed themes, to weld these into an improvised piano accompaniment, but this must follow the work of the patients, not lead it or drag it along!

If the group has already become accustomed to the rhythm band concept rather than creative therapy, then there may be difficulty in establishing the new approach, but it is worth while persevering.

As in most of our therapeutic endeavours, we walk a constant tightrope between expecting too much and expecting too little from our clients. Part of the skill of the therapist is to decide who needs instant success and who needs to have more asked of him, and how we are to plan our programmes to achieve these goals. In working with persons suffering from a dementing process, we are more likely to need to provide easy success and easy achievements, because we are looking at a process which is necessarily downhill. But this should not prevent us from at least presenting new ideas, whilst at the same time being willing to see our plans come to nothing if this is in the best interests of the individual or the group.

Creativity may be seen as a major innovative and cognitive achievement of the human spirit, suitable only for those who are cognitively intact, but we must not perceive the minor creativity of the dementing person as valueless in terms of that person's happiness.

(See also Chapter 9, on Resources, for further thoughts on the choice of musical instruments.)

CHAPTER 7

THE DEMENTING SUFFERER AND THE FAMILY

Supporting the Family in an Institutional Situation

Illness is a family affair!

This may seem so obvious as to need no reiteration, but it is a concept which is of relatively recent origin, and one which is all-too-often forgotten in the busy world of acute hospital medicine. But nowhere is it more true than in dementia, assuming that there is a family to be affected[1,2] There is not always a family, and some of the people who most tug at the heart-strings of the helper are those who have literally no one to care about them apart from professional carers.

As in many conditions, it is probably the "untimely" disease which seems to cause most trauma. Thus the death from cancer of a child, whose life is unfulfilled except to a relatively minor extent, often seems to cause more sadness than the death from cancer of an elderly person who is seen as having lived out most of his life plans and relationships.

Similarly, dementia which has its onset in middle-age is usually more grief-laden than dementia in a very elderly person. (See Chapter 1 for discussion of nomenclature of the dementias, especially as it relates to age of onset.)

We must expect, in the opinion of the author, to see more complicated grief, grief exacerbated by extreme feelings of anger, in relatives of the younger dementing person than in the relatives of the very old. There are, however, limitations to this statement. For example, one cannot fail to be moved by the anguish of the elderly husband who sits each day at the bedside of his equally-old wife who does not recognise that he is there.

But the loss of expectation and the role reversal[3] coupled with the questions, "Why ? Why me? Why us?" are enormously painful. The author was involved in work with a patient and spouse in such a situation. The man was afflicted by severe dementia in middle age, in the midst of the most creative and financially-productive years of his life, and at a time when the couple had been looking forward to a new way of life free from the financial and social responsibility for their children.

In music therapy, the wife was able to enjoy a shared experience of music with her husband despite his advanced dementia. They had met through an amateur musical group and had fallen in love whilst playing opposite each other in a suburban production of a musical, and he responded strongly to the music from that show. This provided only one small comfort to them both. It caused pain as well, but the wife felt that the joy of seeing her husband once more relating to her as he used to do compensated her for the sense of loss which this response also brought.

She was able to deal with some of her anger in fighting for better recognition by government authorities of the needs of younger dementing persons, but again this was only a partial answer for her. She also spoke of the problems her husband's dementia caused to the children when the condition had not been diagnosed. His forgetfulness, irritability (leading sometimes to uncontrollable outbursts of violent behaviour, quite out of keeping with his previous equable, kindly temperament), and incontinence, had caused shame, resentment and social isolation to the young adult children at an age when they wished to bring their friends home and were in the process of developing long-term relationships leading to marriage.

Thus she had a feeling of resentment - initially with her husband, but subsequently with the medical profession for failing to recognise what was happening in him and failing to explain things to her. She also had fears as to the lasting consequences to her young adult family of the traumatic experiences of violence in the early stages of her husband's dementia, as well as fears re the hereditary nature of the condition, in that there is a suspicion that early-onset dementia may have a family incidence. (Early onset

---

[1]Gwyther L.P. & Matteson M.A. "Care for the caregiver." *Jnl. Geront. Nursing*, Feb. 1983, 8, pp 93-95 & 110.

[2]Wilder D.E. et al "Family burden & dementia" in *the dementias*, Raven Press series. (op cit.) pp 239-251.

[3]Bright R. *Grieving*, 1986, M.M.B., USA, p. 13.

Alzheimer's dementia is now commonly referred to as Type 2 and later onset as Type 1)[4]

She also felt guilty when she remembered her angry responses to his changed behaviour, before his condition was diagnosed, feeling that she should have realised that he could not help it, that he was ill and not just violent and strange.

Every family has its own individual problems and its own individual needs in grief, but the family here described demonstrates the complexity of the effects of dementia upon a family and the way in which it can affect two or more generations.

In one such instance, the author was involved in a family interview in which the central figure, the patient, was a woman who was 57 years old, and the others in the interview were her 88-year-old mother, her daughter and her grandchild. The patient was suffering from advanced alcohol-related brain damage, closely akin to dementia, and the family problems consequent upon this were a tangled web of grief, guilt, ambivalence and denial:

- The daughter's marriage was on the verge of breaking up, apparently because she was torn between loyalties to her mother, to her husband and to her child. She wondered whether her life being centred on her marriage and her toddler had contributed to her mother's alcoholism, but at the same time she appeared to be denying that her extreme loyalty to her mother seemed to be responsible for the rapidly-approaching dissolution of that marriage. At the same time, we, as observers, had to consider that her marriage might be failing anyway, even without the problem with her mother, and that possibly visiting her mother and having her to stay was giving her a socially-acceptable reason for avoiding looking at the real issues in her marriage, so that what appeared to be denial was in fact a defence against looking at the marriage, with all the pain that such a process involves.

- The elderly mother was grief-stricken at what had happened in her middle-aged daughter's life, added to which was the usual guilt - "Where did I go wrong that my daughter could end up like this?" She too was torn between loyalty to her impaired daughter and loyalty to her (2nd) husband, the step-father of the patient, who did not want her to come to live in their house. Added to her grief was an extra sense of guilt, in that she wondered whether it was her re-marriage, after her first husband's leaving her, that had contributed to her daughter's alcoholism.

- The small girl was suffering from behaviour problems, presumably reflecting the constant strain of the home and the tensions of relationships.

- The middle-aged alcoholic patient was very largely incapable of understanding anything which was going on, neither the conflict experienced by the mother or the mother's husband, nor by her daughter in her marriage difficulties, nor the effects on the little girl, nor on the father of that child - her daughter's husband.

The precise details of techniques used are immaterial to the present discussion (In general terms they used the child's interest in music as a non-threatening focus for attention and gradually moved the focus from the child to the conflicts which the child's behaviour reflected, conflicts which were breaking the family apart.), but the main direction was important - to try to absolve the family members from their guilt, facilitate their decision to reduce their visiting and to change the constant focus of all their emotional energies and attention from the impaired patient to their own families, and deal with any problems there.

It was important that this should be done without any punitive overtones, to ensure that they were not seeing their reduction of care as punishing her for being an alcoholic, but simply as a shift of loyalties from an over-emphasis on the patient to adequate emphasis on their own relationships.

There is a parallel to this in many of the relationships which we see at second-hand, and it is vital that nursing and other staff make notes of the extent of visiting, of any signs of stress and burn-out which they observe in relatives, and encourage the relatives to talk about what it is like to have a dementing family

[4]McLean S. "Assessing dementia, Part II: clinical, functional, neuropsychological and social issues" *Australia and New Zealand journal of psychiatry,* 1987, **21**, pp 284-304

member. This is not to be seen as prying into personal relationships which are nothing to do with us, but rather as an extension of the concepts of community care, in which the patient may be the focus of attention but in which the whole family system is seen as being at risk in chronic illness, disability and despair.

Through music we not only reach the sufferer but his relatives too, giving to them a sense of usefulness which is often lost in the institutional care of dementing persons. We can ask what music the relative used to enjoy, and then play this, even if it brings overt grief. We need to fore-arm relatives about this, reassuring them that it is OK to cry, that music can produce simultaneously both grief and happiness, and so on.

The group music session, followed by private conversation with relatives, is an ideal situation in which to build up the strengths of relatives. We can allow them to ventilate grief and anger (with the person concerned, with God, with society for not providing better and more-readily-available care for dementing persons), their guilt with themselves for feeling resentful at the financial cost of care, about the disruption to their personal lives, guilt for wanting to be out of it and free, for longing for the person to die - but then feeling more guilty about this, especially experiencing guilt finally about their feelings of relief when he does die, and so on.

We must have expert knowledge about the dementing processes which may be taking place in the patient, what the prognosis is - as far as anyone can possibly know - as well as deep understanding of the kind of emotions they will be feeling at this time. For relatives to be told that we meet many people who long for the dementing sufferer to hurry up and die can be very comforting to those who are guiltily trying to deny such thoughts! Similarly we must be able to help them cope with their feelings of resentment over the costs of long-term care, resentment over the changes to personal life-plans which dementia in a relative causes, anger with the medical profession for not being able to cure the disease, resentment over the way they themselves may have been treated in the early stages of the disease when requests for help brought little useful response. These and many other responses are commonplace amongst relatives of dementing persons, and it is vital if we are to bring them any comfort and tranquillity that they are reassured that it is not "bad" to feel like this, that such reactions are normal.

When relatives do distance themselves from the patient, e.g., by saying, "He has a good life, and he is so lost in his own little world that he does not need me," or, "He does not recognise me when I come so why do I need to come all this way to see him?", it is hard to avoid feeling annoyed and disappointed, and it can be helpful to remind ourselves that we do not really know the full background. The person who seems to us a pathetic, helpless individual in need of T.L.C. may have been a bullying, demanding person who made no effort to cause his family to love him, and their failure to visit may be the direct consequence of his earlier actions towards them.

On the other hand, such defences may be a vital method of surviving the painful experience of seeing a person one has known, loved and respected, changed into an incontinent, mumbling, wandering and almost-unrecognisable patient, quite different from the person we once knew. Gosling has written[5] of "Mourners without a death" and her remarks are as applicable to the relatives and friends of a person with advanced dementing syndrome as they are for brain-damaged victims of car accidents .

But denial of such feelings is not a healthy way of dealing with them. People may need an enormous amount of support and building of self-esteem before they can acknowledge that they are longing for their demented mother to die, and yet when they can be helped to acknowledge this, and be reassured that most people - even staff - may feel like this, the open-ness and honesty in itself brings healing in way which denial and pretence can never do.

We need to have a number of different ways of expressing things, according to the social nuances which we observe in the relatives.

---

[5]Gosling P. "Mourners without a death." *Brit. Jnl. Psychiat.* 1980, **137**, pp 397-398.

For example:

(In an early dementia) "It must be so humiliating for your father, who has always been a professional man, to realise that he can no longer remember things. And upsetting for you too, to see it happening."

(In a later stage) "I feel really sad sometimes when I watch your mother trying to feed herself, and think back to what she must have been like when you were children, running the family life and being so practical in everything."

(In any stage of dementia) "Your husband has always been such a strong man, using his strength in his daily work, you must be unhappy to see him so helpless, and wonder WHY it happens like this!"

As professionals we often need to give permission to relatives to cut down on the number and length of their visits, if it seems that they are held to their visiting patterns by guilt, or if it is clear that their own family needs should take first place, or that their own health is suffering from the strain of visiting.

"I know your family life has been difficult recently, I hope you will feel it is OK just to come in for a short time once a week. Your family at home really needs you right now, and we do give your grandfather a lot of tender loving care, even though we are a nursing home! We notice that although he cries each time you go and says 'Take me home with you', he settles down again as soon as you are out of sight, so you don't need to feel too awful about leaving him."

Perhaps the most difficult person to help is the spouse in a marriage which we know has been extremely unhappy or the adult "child" of a difficult and demanding or over-protective parent, who continues (out of guilt?) to visit over-frequently.

In such instances, we may get the feeling that the spouse or child needs permission to cut down on the visiting, and for them to know that we understand a little how they feel may provide the permission which is needed. Some relatives need this permission to come from the doctor because he/she is perceived as having more authority.

"It must be difficult for you, coming all this way. From little things I notice about him, I often have the feeling that your husband (wife, mother, father) has not always been an easy person to live with!"

We can hope that this opening remark may lead on to a useful conversation, which will help the unhappy spouse or child to make a decision about visiting, without being unduly influenced by guilty feelings.

Obviously these are not set phrases to be learned off like a parrot, but they do give useful ideas as to how reassurance can be expressed without leading relatives to feel useless and unwanted, and to assure them that we do have some idea of how they feel, even though no one can truly know except the person who is in the relationship.

We need knowledge also to help those relatives, especially the spouse, who observe the quasi-normal behaviour and responses of a dementing person in a music group and who are led - because of these responses - to think that there is a chance of substantial improvement, even of getting better altogether.

In one such instance, in which there was irremediable dementia because of a series of strokes, the husband became so optimistic of his wife's total recovery because of the way she responded to Jewish music of their shared background, that it was necessary, after discussion in the team as well as with the husband, to discontinue his involvement in the music therapy. "It is great to see your wife joining in the music sessions, but unfortunately we find that this does not necessarily mean that she will get back completely to how she used to be before she started to have these strokes."

Ideally we should perceive family counselling as including the sufferer; the person suffering from dementia is, in the early stages, aware that something is wrong, although he may not know exactly what is happening, and he tends to feel isolated and afraid.

Much of our work is necessarily done with the sufferer himself, because of difficulties for relatives in visiting during working hours, but we must always perceive the sufferer as a member of a family even if that "family" consists only of fellow-residents and staff of a retirement community or home.

Grief for the family may be easy to approach or it may be difficult. This will depend upon the private hang-ups of the relatives, their feelings of guilt at having put the person into a home or other institution, whether or not they feel they have contributed to his dementia and so on. For example, family members may fear that the person has become demented because they have not visited him enough, not checked up on his nutrition or his general health sufficiently, and so on. Such guilty feelings may be entirely irrational, but may nevertheless influence their behaviour to patient and staff.

We must be so attuned as to avoid intrusive trampling upon hidden feelings and hurts, which may date back a generation or more, but which may be as immediate as that morning, when, for example, the visitor's wife may have said, "If you go out to that home to see your mother one more Saturday instead of coming out with me, I'm leaving!" On the other hand, when we work by means of music with patient and family together, as a joint activity, an atmosphere of trust develops readily and it is then easier for us to broach such painful topics as family conflicts, guilt and embarrassment over the dementia and over the admission, etc.

Ideally such reassurance should be a matter of team support, but, if the trust is a fragile thing, then initially we may have to work alone. All we can do is to try to give relatives permission to express their feelings, reassure them as much as is in our power, build up a sense of trust in the staff as a whole, and then pass them on to social worker, physician or whoever is appropriate for further discussion, when they are willing to talk to someone else.

Grieving for the sufferer is hard to assess, as so much depends on the level of cognitive functioning which is retained. All we can do is be as observant as we can of responses to music and to conversation. We must observe family relationships as they are revealed in a music session, either individually or in a group, and work co-operatively with other staff.

One of the fears of the dementing sufferer is that of becoming "insane", because of the old belief, commonly held even today, that any problem connected with the mind is a form of madness.

Even if the person himself appears to be incapable of grasping the deeper meaning of what we say we must reassure him: "You are still you, you are still a person, we care about you and will do everything we can to make life pleasant for you. It must be scary for you to find yourself forgetting things and people, but it is not your fault, it is an illness called Alzheimer's disease."

When one adopts this approach it is surprising (or is it?!) to see how deep and alive a response we elicit. In the opinion of the author, such conversation should be prefaced by music, in order to build rapport and initiate cognitive functioning to the highest possible level, and - having done this - the time is ripe to speak openly, acknowledging the dementia as a disease, offering comfort and caring. If the relative is present, so much the better, but it is necessary to repeat these remarks on a number of occasions so it is not of great moment if, from time to time, one has to work without the presence of relatives.

The accessibility of self-help groups is of great support for relatives in coping with their living grief, and we must know how to put relatives in touch with such groups, having information booklets available so that thought may lead to action. Those who are worn down by grieving and constant anxiety may not be able to make the effort for themselves to find out an address, but to have the information readily available takes one extra task away. At the same time we leave the decision to the person concerned whether or not she will act upon the information, so that we continue to foster independence rather than dependency states.

When working with the family and sufferer together, it is helpful to bear in mind that any chronic illness or disability is likely to have similar effects on the whole circle of Significant Others - relatives and close friends - effects which may have outcome for years to come. By our intervention it may be possible to de-fuse some of the guilts and consequences of grief, so that we thereby may hope to reduce those long-term effects.

The Dementing Person and the Family at Home

Some elderly dementing persons can, in the early stages of the condition, remain at home even if there are no relatives in the house to support them. This capacity for home life is usually dependent upon the provision of domiciliary nursing visits, Meals on Wheels and so on, but may be possible simply with the help of supportive neighbours. One morning, when making a home visit to such a person living in complete isolation, the author arrived at the door carrying a musical instrument, to have the door almost slammed as she approached, the woman saying, "No, thank you, not today, I don't need any musical instruments today!" However after some persuasion entry was permitted and there followed a pleasant half-hour visit with music, singing and conversation.

The conditions under which she was living by her own choice, were (to the outsider) chaotic in that she had all the contents of her drawers piled up on the beds and she slept on the couch downstairs.

The total cleanliness of the house was questionable, but there was no danger in the way she lived, she was extremely careful of fire, gas, matches and heaters. She was fortunate in that her neighbours appeared proud rather than otherwise of her "dottiness" and were willing to support her determination to stay at home. The attitude of neighbours is usually crucial to such decisions, and if we care about the freedom of the individual, this must include the freedom to take risks and live alone in a mess rather than tidily in an institution, so long as the person is in any way capable of making a decision. But sometimes the neighbours exert so much pressure that the individual loses the precious gift of freedom. True, there are risks attached, and we have to weigh up the dangers against the freedom! However, usually it is difficult for the person suffering from moderate dementia, who lacks a family, to be able to stay at home.

There is today an increasing emphasis on home care in early dementia when there is a family to provide support, in order to avoid premature admission to an institution. There are obvious advantages in this - the individual retains links with familiar surroundings, his family and neighbours, he functions better at home because of the familiarity and the family does not feel the guilt which is commonly experienced when admission to an institution is effected. But, since dementia is a continuing process, these feelings of guilt - unjustified though they may be are only delayed, because admission will almost certainly be required eventually.

There are, however, many burdens which the family has to bear when a decision is made to keep the dementing relative at home in a joint menage:

- Constant watchfulness, so that the carers can never entirely relax (because of the risks of fire, the hazards of being locked out of the house by the anxious dementing person who locks every door she passes, the need to cope with problems of incontinence, and so on.)
- Needing to arrange "Granny sitters", or support through a Day Centre, when an outing of any kind is planned.
- The need for respite residential care so that the carers may have a complete holiday from time to time.
- Frequent anxiety about health - "Is this just a minor cold in the nose or should we seek professional help?" "Is she getting worse?" " What should we be doing for her?"
- Loss of privacy in the constant intrusion by a dementing person into every room, every conversation. (Especially difficult for the adult child of a dementing person, the more so if his/her marriage is under stress.)
- Loss of sleep when there is a change in day/night behaviour due to increasing dementia.
- Tolerance of repeated questions, perhaps accusations, or criticisms of the way things are done.
- The attitudes of friends who may be less enthusiastic about visiting the home because of the presence of a dementing person.

- The difficulty of coping with home care out of a sense of duty, when the dementing person has throughout his or her life been difficult, demanding or disruptive to family life.

- The possible risk of alienation of young adult children who sometimes leave home because of the dementia of a resident grandparent, especially if the dementia includes accusations and/or "dirty" behaviour with food, incontinence and so on.

- The sadness of seeing, on a daily, hourly basis, the deterioration of a loved person.

- Difficulties in making a decision as to when home care is no longer possible, and then finding suitable, affordable accommodation.

- Coping with the guilt when this decision has been made, or when they find themselves thinking "I wonder how much longer this will go on, when she will die..."

These and others difficulties (depending on the patterns of family life, the personality and the past relationships of the family with the relative, and so on) may constitute a very real burden, but are not sufficient in many instances to prevent people from caring at home for their dementing parents, spouse or other relative, and from finding happiness in so doing.

But support is often needed, even if it is not actively sought, and neighbours, church congregations, community groups, service clubs etc will be possibly be able to offer help. This will include emotional support, reassuring the family that the dementing person is still respected despite his illness, that the dementia is recognised by the community as an illness which can happen to anyone - that it is not seen as reprehensible. In Australia and elsewhere, many churches, Lawn Bowls Clubs and other sporting and/or social groups provide outings and enjoyment for demented members, arranging visits to the church or club in which the sufferer is welcomed as still worthwhile, still a friend, and - in church worship - has his or her spiritual as well as social needs satisfied.

At the same time the visits offer the family a half-day of freedom to be themselves without anxiety over the welfare of the relative.

Professional support services will probably also be needed by the family, and these, of course, depend upon the domiciliary services which are supplied by statutory or local authorities.

Services needed will probably include :

- Linen service for bedclothes, in case of incontinence.

- Provision of equipment - commode, bedpans or bottles, hoists for lifting heavy sufferers in and out of bed, wheelchairs etc.

- Home nursing help for bathing, injections etc.

- Somebody to stay with the sufferer while the carer does shopping and personal activities.

- Home visits for podiatry, physiotherapy as required.

For many families, enormous emotional and practical support is provided by the regular assessment and re-assessment of the dementing person by the area geriatrician, in which the family's coping strategies and emotional health will also be quietly observed. Appropriate guidance can then be given, when the time comes, to enable the family to place the dementing person in residential accommodation without undue guilt.

For some relatives it will be necessary for a visiting professional actually to make the decision as to institutional care, in order to absolve the family members from the extremes of guilt when home care is no longer feasible.

Such regular visits also ensure that unnecessary suffering is not endured by the dementing person. It is common for all problems to be ascribed to the dementing process, when in fact some of the health problems may respond well to treatment. For example, because incontinence is a feature of advanced dementia, families often assume that to have a relative suddenly become incontinent is simply part of their dementing process. It may, however, be caused by a urinary tract infection, which will respond well to treatment with appropriate medication, and the "incontinence" is rapidly cured!

In many places there are day centres for the care of dementing persons, where care is given for one, two or three days a week either free or at a nominal cost, and - so long as major sleep patterns have not been changed, with major day/night reversal which would adversely affect day care - such centres do enable the family to continue to care for the person at home. And to keep the dementing person busy through the day may, in any case, help to maintain or restore normal circadian rhythms.

At day care centres music is usually included because of the recognised response to music of dementing persons, and families who seek day care for a relative should ask about the way in which music programmes are provided and organised.

Relatives may feel diffident about making enquiries about such matters, but ideally those who are arranging for day care (or who, later on, are looking for residential care) should seek assurance that the music groups meet the needs of the client.

In summary, the needs which are frequently ignored are :

- The need for the music to be personally presented - recorded music coming from a machine with no human intervention, no introduction, no opportunity for discussion etc, is anti-therapeutic in that it contributes to the de-personalising process.
- The need to have sadness accepted and tolerated for some of the time, without this sadness being seen by the organisers or other staff as a reflection upon their competence. (There have been many instances of the person running a music group feeling apprehensive if someone cries, in case the management of the nursing home or day centre perceives this as a failure.)
- The need for balance to be maintained between music as fun and music which recognises the emotions of the client and his family.
- The need for cognitive stimulation to ensure that functioning is maintained at the best possible level.
- But, at the same time, there is a need to avoid imposing unreal expectations and consequent strains upon the individual.
- The need for the family being permitted to participate in the music sessions, if they wish to do so, in order to help maintain family relationships.

Music in the Home

Many people feel able to arrange music sessions at home as a family affair, involving a dementing relative. The music which is chosen will depend upon the taste and preference of the family as a whole but with the preference of the dementing person as paramount.

In some families there is joy in singing hymns or old popular songs together, in the way which used to be popular in the pre-television days of Sunday evening singalongs around the piano or pianola (player-piano). (Some books which contain suitable music are listed in the final chapter, headed "Resources".)

In some parts of the world, home visits by the music therapist are encouraged or at least permitted, and the challenge to the therapist is substantial. We should aim to involve the spouse or the adult child in the sessions, since for many families it is only through music that they see a (temporary) restoration of the person they once knew. Mention has already been made (See Chapter 3.) of the fact that it is the change, from an active involved person to an apathetic one, that families find most distressing, so that to provide an environment in which the personality of the dementing person is restored, even if only for a few minutes, is a source of joy to the family.

We may see sadness, but grieving is only destructive if we leave people alone to cope as best they may, without support and counselling.

How much help the family can be given in the provision of musical equipment will depend - as so many aspects of health care depend - upon the provision of finances for health care of the elderly, and how far music therapy is perceived as an essential part of such services, with home visits as well as institutional programmes.

One helpful system is for an area health service or a base hospital to have a number of tape recorders and a library of tapes for loan and use in families where there is a dementing person. The Red Cross in Australia has for many years provided library services of recorded music for small institutions which do not have sufficient funds to provide their own resources, and one can envisage the extension of such services to families.

In the Royal Victoria Hospital, Montreal, the Palliative Care unit has musical equipment which is lent to families as part of the home care programme. Although this is concerned with terminal illness rather than dementia, there is no fundamental reason why any large well-funded hospital should not set up the same system for families who are linked to the establishment in a home care programme for demented persons. Recorded music is not the perfect medium for music stimulation but it does help the family who otherwise feel themselves to be incompetent, and they can be given guidance as to the use of recorded music. For example, one would recommend that the music is chosen from pieces known to be familiar, that the carer and the dementing person listen to the music together for a short time, then try to talk a little about what has been heard, using other stimuli as well, such as family photographs.

One would encourage the carer to sing familiar songs or hymns when alone with the sufferer, even if she feels that she is too self-conscious to do it in public. Choose some dance music if dancing has been part of the person's life, and encourage the carer, especially if this is the spouse, to dance gently for a few minutes, and talk about "Do you remember when we used to..." All these activities should only be carried out for ten to fifteen minutes; despite this brief time, it will be of value in maintaining a sense of the sufferer as the person he used to be.

In the book *The Thirty Six Hour Day* there are helpful suggestions as to how music may be used, for example in encouraging the dementing person to stay on the toilet for long enough for a bladder or bowel motion to occur. But although one should not assume that this will be effective each time, or for an extended period of time, it may make the difference between the carer being able or unable to cope with problems of incontinence. (See recommended reading list in Appendix.)

One would recommend that a variety of favourite pieces of music should be used for a toileting programme rather than using one piece only, since there would be, one assumes, a slight risk of setting up a Pavlovian type of conditioned reflex, so that hearing a particular piece of music led to emptying of bowel or bladder. Whilst this is useful at home, it could cause difficulties if one were out somewhere and the chance hearing of that piece of music elicited the toilet response.

Much can be done to enable those families which wish to keep a dementing relative at home to do so, but we must also be ready to provide support for those who have reached the end of their tether to make a decision for nursing home or other institutional care. The music therapist who is making home visits needs sufficient knowledge and empathy to assist the family when this need arises.

CHAPTER 8

MUSIC FOR RECREATION AND FUN

A recurring question concerns the similarities and differences between music as recreation and music as therapy.

Probably each of us has a somewhat different attitude about this, but that of the author is as follows.

To be classified as " Music Therapy," the programme must :

- Be planned with the needs of each individual in mind including his diagnosis, overall treatment plans, the expectations of the whole team as to what may be achieved both in general terms, as regards the music and the integration between the music and the total treatment plan.

- Include a music therapy assessment, even if this has to be simple in the extreme, as in advanced dementia. Depending on assessments made by others, and the reliability of these, it may also include a general assessment by the music therapist of the mood as observed in music sessions, family relationships and so on.

- Include record-keeping so as to keep as far as possible an objective account of what has taken place and responses to the individual sessions. The Problem Orientated method is eminently suited to record keeping in music therapy. (See Chapter 2.)

- Include evaluation of the outcome of our interventions, with adjustment and change as this becomes necessary.

- Encompass team consultation so that work in music therapy is integrated with that of other professions, and knowledge of responses to music is included in general assessment, planning of placement on a long-term basis, and so on.

- Include some kind of record-keeping even when working with a group, noting interactions and group dynamics; the group should be small enough that individual responses can also be noted with some degree of accuracy.

It is recognised that recreational music may lack all or most of these requirements and yet still have a healing influence upon the unhappy, socially isolated individual. The therapeutic spin-off (as the author usually describes it) is, however, partly a matter of chance in that no specific plans are drawn up to make the music programme fit the general treatment needs and plans for the individuals.

It is true that in many countries music therapy as a profession has had its origins in recreational music - for example in observations made of the responses of psychiatric patients to concerts or to individual music-making. But this is no longer adequate as constituting an up-to-date concept of music therapy. We need to be accountable for what takes place with our clients, and document our work so that others may know what has been happening and also so that results may be seen to be replicable.

Despite all this, the establishment which has been set up to care for dementing persons, and which cannot employ a "proper" music therapist is likely to use music for the recreational needs of its clients. This will probably be of benefit to those clients, but only so long as certain principles are recognised and observed:

1. That music does not necessarily induce euphoria but may elicit the deepest feelings of grief and anger.

2. Failure to meet those needs in an empathic manner is a dereliction of professional duty.

3. The individualism of the client must be respected, despite his dementia, and to "opt out" of a music session is his inalienable right, even if he is unable to explain why he wishes to leave. He may choose to return, and may reasonably have some gentle persuasion offered to achieve this, but that is all.

4. Recognition of the individual means that we must cater for a wide variety of musical tastes. Because a dementing person is unable to express his preference, this does not mean that he must enjoy "pub" or "party" singalong music; he may have had a life history of professional music-making or taste which makes such music intolerable.

5. Music sessions should not consist of singing through a set routine of songs - one can be institutionalised on a series of song sheets as easily as on a regimented routine of any other kind. Nor should music be provided merely in recordings, it must be consist mainly of "live" music for best effect, even though some records are used for special purposes.

6. Playing musical instruments must be a matter of choice, they must not be thrust into unwilling hands without empathic efforts to see whether they are acceptable.

7. So-called "Rhythm Band," the simple hitting of drums, tambourines etc in time to a record or accompaniment, is not very therapeutic in that it fails to meet any latent creativity. This must not be neglected, even though creativity may be well hidden or even prove to be lost in the demented client. If it is indeed lost, then the rhythmic playing of instruments without any differentiation between types of music may be all that one can hope for.

8. Efforts must be made to provide separate levels of musical experience for persons with differing cognitive abilities.

9. Groups must be kept small; music is not an easy, cheap way of providing an acceptable activity for large numbers of people simultaneously. There may be a cosmetic effect in presenting an institution as having a good programme, but if the needs of the clients are truly paramount, then groups of demented persons must not exceed 5 or 6, with, if other staff are available to help, perhaps up to 10 or 12. If numbers are higher, there is no prospect of true participation for dementing persons, with their impaired powers of concentration, observation and communication, in addition to the sensory losses seen in dementia and/or old age - visual, auditory, perceptual losses and so on.

10. Adequate numbers of staff must be involved; a music session does not provide an opportunity for other members of staff to have a coffee break, leaving one hapless volunteer or diversional/recreational therapist to run the programme alone. (See 9, above.) This is particularly important because of the prevalence of incontinence - staff must be available to take people to the toilet before the session begins, and through the session if required. There will probably be no request for the toilet, but restlessness is often a useful pointer.

(See Chapter 7 on the needs which may be neglected in music recreation programmes.)

Many of these remarks, e.g., about size of groups, availability of staff to assist especially in toileting, apply as much to music therapy as to music recreation. But one would assume that, in music therapy planning, there is no need to emphasise these matters.

These comments are outspoken to the point of bluntness, but the author has seen too many nursing homes with so-called programmes of music therapy, inflicting boredom and humiliation upon a significant number of the participants, to be evasive in making these concepts as clear as is possible in print!

True recreation is of therapeutic benefit to the individual. How many of us, when feeling "down" have found playing a loved piece of music helps us feel more serene? It may be that the sense of order transmitted by the music gives us a sense of order and peace in our lives, or the tempestuous nature of another piece may express for us the stormy relationship which is worrying us and yet bring it under control. These and other responses led, in the early days of music therapy, to a recognition of the power of music to heal, and they are still true today. But with persons who have dementing conditions, it is harder to ensure that the music will be helpful unless one knows of the person's preferences from an outside agency. (See previous chapter on work with the family.)

Given the prospect of preparing a programme of recreational music for a group of dementing persons, one would aim to have a variety of types of music, including, for example:

- a Strauss waltz,
- a melody from a musical comedy, the choice depending on the ages of the participants,
- some well-known songs so that people can join in the words as well as the melody; they may or may not include favourite hymns, depending upon the group, and may be sung as a "bracket" or interspersed through the programme. (See note below.)
- some short excerpt of "serious" music such as a song by Schubert, a Chopin piano piece, an excerpt from a classical ballet such as Tchaikowsky's *Sleeping Beauty*,
- a Sousa march, which could incorporate a band segment.

The pieces (some of which could be recorded but some should be played "live") would be interspersed with songs of the appropriate era. (If no information is available, use the clients' ages to guess as to what will be familiar, by playing music which was popular when they were in their early adult life.) Include some music from other countries if you have migrants in the group, and make sure that the programme is not too long; 45 minutes is the most which would be possible, and this would be for a group of early-sufferers only. Have a small number of musical instruments of good quality, make a gentle offer of an instrument, with no insistence that it be accepted or put them on tables in front of participants, to be picked up only if the person wishes to do so, but be ready to help them hold things correctly if there is any sign of interest.

If sessions are planned with understanding and respect for the participants, then a recreational session will bring benefit in terms of enjoyment and fun. Since fun is lamentably deficient in most institutions or units for dementing persons, the provision of enjoyment is of itself valuable! Empathy is needed to ensure that confusion is not heightened by any programme. For example, "Let's pretend" sessions in which a mock wedding takes place, may result in needless distress and confusion if the events are half-remembered but not understood as make-believe.

It is, however, usually acceptable to introduce music by saying, "Let's pretend we are going for a picnic" or, "Let's think what it used to be like to dance at a ball", and even if one or two persons do think that they are actually going to a dance, little harm will be done. They may be able to live out their imaginings by getting up and dancing, and no adverse after-effects are likely to occur.

Summing it up, one may say that recreational music will, if well planned and carried out, provide therapeutic spin-off as well as pleasure, and music therapy, if well planned and carried out, will provide fun and laughter as well as treatment. The main requirements are that the organisers have empathy with the difficulties faced by their clients and their families and also have practical music skills which will permit the music groups to have life and energy.

CHAPTER 9

RESOURCES

Resources required for a music therapy programme include people, with appropriate talents and skills, and equipment.

"People" include the skills of the people, and for music therapy these cover two main areas: personal skills and gifts, and music skills.

Personal Skills

- A willingness to acquire the basic knowledge of the conditions with which we are working, in terms of physical, intellectual, social, emotional and spiritual health, i.e. what the dementia means to the sufferer and the family.

- Self-knowledge, to understand one's own responses to helplessness, to the possibly unattractive appearance of our clients, to their difficult behaviour, and to the inexorable downward path, since this makes demands upon the therapist that are not made by conditions where improvement can be expected.

- A capacity for unselfconscious fun and enjoyment, the gift of rejoicing in small gains, of seeing hope where the outsider may see only despair, the courage to weep with those who weep but also to laugh with those who find laughter in surprising places! Also to accept people as they are, enjoying their positive attributes and ignoring the unattractive aspects.

Music Therapy is not all solemnity and science; even though we need to look objectively at what we are doing, for the sake of our clients, we also need an ability to enjoy life in general and what we do in particular!

Music Skills

We need:

- Practical gifts so that we can play an appropriate accompanying instrument, play music to be listened to, play melodies by ear with keyboard accompaniment after hearing them sung by a relative or by a patient. The instrument chosen may be a piano, portable keyboard, piano accordion, autoharp or guitar, but we must remember that the autoharp and guitar give only a small volume of sound, which makes them inappropriate for the individual who is hearing-impaired or for any group with more than five elderly people.

- Other music skills, which include sightreading, and transposition at sight, since many songbooks include music written in a totally inappropriate key, and one must be able at sight to put things up or down (usually down!) without there being any delay whilst one works out the chords.

- The skills which enable us to create instant accompaniment from a melody line with or without chords written above, since many of the most useful books of songs give only these basic items of information.

- Extensive knowledge of a large repertoire of music of all types, because in a dementia unit one may meet one client who has been a professional opera singer, another whose experience of music is limited to the church choir, another whose choice is ballroom dancing music of the 1930's, another who has been a musicologist specialising in pre-Bach music, and so on.

Equipment

This must include a portable accompanying instrument; the modern electronic keyboard, with its versatility in reproducing with reasonable authenticity the sound of several instruments, plus a convincing rhythmic bass, is useful. The author has long used a piano accordion because of its portable nature, but it does somewhat restrict one in the type of music which can be played, although the fact that it can be taken anywhere, without a need for electric power, may outweigh the disadvantages.

The guitar is favoured by some therapists, but is not always appropriate for the severely demented client who has hearing losses, or for the person who feels unfamiliar with the instrument, as may occur because of memory failure.

A battery-operated tape recorder is useful, because it can freely be moved around a group to reach those who need direct contact with the instrument itself, either because of inattention or hearing deficits. To go with the tape instrument, one needs a large library of recorded music, as a supplement to the general work in "live" music which forms the backbone of any programme of music therapy. It is useful, too, for recording patients singing etc. for future use.

We should plan on including in our tape library:

- Items from the classical symphonic repertoire such as Mozart, Beethoven and Brahms.
- Lighter classical pieces, such as Strauss waltzes, Franz Lehar, Chopin waltzes.
- Ballet music, e.g., Tchaikowsky's *Sleeping Beauty* and *Swan Lake*, Chopin's *Les Sylphides.*
- Operatic excerpts, preferably sung by singers known to our clients from their younger days. Many composite recordings can be purchased, or one may select excerpts from total opera recordings.
- Dance music - ballroom dances, folk dances of appropriate ethnic origin, depending on the background of our potential clientele.
- Excerpts from musical comedies such as *Rose Marie, Maid of the Mountains*, as well as more recent shows such as *South Pacific, Sound of Music, My Fair Lady* and so on.
- Film themes; again composite recordings can be purchased.
- Local music (e.g., Outback folk songs in Australia, and so on.)

To have these readily available means that there is an interesting tonal contrast in the music played, that it is not ALL piano music, or ALL organ music, but we are stimulated by the variety of tonal colour from an orchestra and by singers whose voices are familiar (e.g., Paul Robeson, Richard Tauber, Gigli, Chaliapin.)

The list above is by no means complete, and each therapist will develop his or her own library depending upon the needs of the people with whom he or she works.

Songbooks

These have already been mentioned above, and there are several useful sources of music to cover a wide variety of age-groups and interests. All of these recommended books have the copyright date of songs printed clearly at the bottom of the page, and these dates, allied perhaps to books of photographs of the era, are useful in starting reminiscence or simply in jogging the memory. "This song was popular about the time you were growing up," etc.

The *Ultimate Fake Book* is excellent in that it has several indices, permitting one to pick out songs for special days, special types of music and so on. The disadvantage is that the book is so large that the spiral plastic binding of the author's copy fell apart and the book had to be completely re-bound in four separate volumes, the index reproduced in each volume, thereby making it more manageable!
(Published in 1981 by the U.S. firm Hal Leonard.)

Many similar books containing an enormous variety of songs with melody and chords plus words of one or two verses are available, such as Albert's *1001 Hit Tunes*. (Available by mail, Music Sales P.O. Box 279, Artarmon, NSW, 2064, Australia.)

Other series contain the entire music of the songs, sometimes chosen at random, but often selected according to a particular era, as in the Musical Memories series (published by Wise Publications) and available from:

Music Sales, in Australia, address as above.
Music Sales, in England, 78, Newman Street, London, WIP 3LA, UK.
Music Sales, in USA, 24, East 22nd Street, New York, NY 10010,USA.

The Musical Memories series covers contains separate books for:
1900 - 1920, 1920 - 1930, 1930 - 1940, 1940 - 1950, 1950 - 1960, 1960 - 1970, 1970 - 1980.
These are particularly useful in that the covers consist of photographs of items in use at the time - radio sets, cameras etc, all indicating the change in design and approach as the century has progressed, and these have been stimulating when added to a programme of music.

The same suppliers also distribute a series called *The Joy of....* including Folk, Jazz & Boogie, Blues, Guitar, Rag-time, Christmas and so on, all of which provide useful resources in planning varied programmes of music to stimulate the memory.

The Readers' Digest songbooks offer an excellent variety of music, especially useful in that each song is headed by a paragraph about the song, who sang it or wrote it, and other information.

The well-known Ulverscroft large print book series includes two large-print songbooks, in both words-only and words-and-music editions. Although the songs in the first (the *Blue Book*) are now really suitable only for the very old (the first edition of songs chosen by the author was published in the late 1960's), many of them may be known to younger persons who heard parents or grandparents singing them. But care must be taken to intersperse songs from this book with others of somewhat more up-to-date provenance; otherwise there may be some unrest in groups, even amongst those who are demented. Kate Baker later arranged the music for non-professional pianists, in large print, with the idea that clients would enjoy playing them, but the professional musician or therapist will readily fill out the simple chord accompaniments to provide a more interesting bass. (See telephone directories in major capital cities for the nearest distributors of Ulverscroft publications.) The second book (bound in red card) published in 1987 has a more up-to-date collection selected by Margaret Donald, C.M.T., who has extensive experience in geriatrics.

Musical Instruments for Our Clients

(Some of the following discussion was included in the section on assessment, in Chapter 2, in the section on promoting Socialising, in Chapter 5, and in Chapter 6 on creativity, but is repeated here for the sake of clarity, in having all the information together under "Resources")

The autoharp is a useful instrument for those who are unaffected by apraxia (i.e., those who can carry out planned movements), since the chord bars can be help down by the therapist and the client can sweep a plectrum across the strings, enjoying the chords which are heard - and also felt, since the vibrations are experienced quite strongly by the player.

Percussion band instruments need to be used with care, but it is helpful to have a good supply of good quality instruments; it is suggested that resources of these should include:

- Bongo drums, several sets.
- Maracas - these vary in weight, and although the larger ones produce a larger tone, the additional weight for frail hands to hold may not justify the extra tonal quality.
- Castanets, the type with a handle are perhaps easier to manage than those which are more authentically Spanish.
- Triangles are not useful unless they are suspended from a metal frame so that only one hand is needed, two handed use is over-complex for the demented client.

- Tambourines are good, because they can either be played "correctly" with two hands or they can be held with one hand and the sound produced by tapping the face of the instrument on the arm of a wheel chair, on one's knee and so on, or by shaking.

- Sleigh bells are light in weight, and have the advantage that a person whose sense of rhythm is impaired can play the bells constantly without the sounds really spoiling the rhythmic effect of those who can still play in time with the music.

- Tone blocks, in which there is a central hollow tube of wood and a beater, each end of the tube giving a different pitch, suffer from the same problem as we see in the triangle. They are only useful for the exceptional patient with minor deficits.

- Drums which require drumsticks may or may not be useful - much will depend upon the cognitive and praxic status of the client concerned. But it would be useful to have one or two drums with sticks, and use them only when there is an appropriate person in the group.

- Cymbals vary in size from very small finger cymbals which fit on the fingers with an elastic band, to heavy orchestral size, with many in between. Persons with some capacity for coordination may enjoy playing them, but anyone who has difficulty with spatial concepts will find them difficult and frustrating to try to use. There may also be difficulties for those in the group who have a hearing problem known as "recruitment", one of the complications of partial deafness in which loud sounds are magnified to the point of pain. So cymbals may be better kept for specific occasions or people rather than routine use.

- The South American instrument known as The Fish, guiro, has had only limited success in the author's experience because most older people fail to perceive the tone produced as having any musical value and hear it simply as a noise. (This opinion has been voiced by nondemented persons, but the author has assumed that the view would be shared by demented persons also.)

- Tuned percussion instruments can be useful for the person who has only a very minor degree of deficit, and some people have been helped in crossing the mid-line by playing a beater on a xylophone or a metallophone from one end to the other. Those who have previously been pianists may find the instrument confusing, but many people enjoy the stimulation and the pleasant sounds, which can stimulate creativity. Some patients are happier with a single chime bar. The author has worked with three pianists who lost their pianistic skills as a result of strokes with some dementia, and they found joy in the metallophone because playing it made use of their musicality but without the constant reminder of their losses that attempting to play the piano caused.

No definite rules can be given as to what resources are essential for music therapy programmes for dementing persons, but the above lists will serve as an approximate guide, to be changed and developed according to the ideas and skills of the therapist concerned and the needs of the people who are receiving therapy individually or in a group.

APPENDIX

BIBLIOGRAPHY

BOOKS ON DEMENTIA OR WHICH INCLUDE INFORMATION ON DEMENTIA, FOR GENERAL REFERENCE AND RESOURCE MATERIAL

N.B. Some of these have already been listed in the References in the footnotes; they are repeated here as in indication of general use, as well as the specific points referred to in the text.

1. Mace N. & Rabins P. — *The thirty-six hour day.* Johns Hopkins, Baltimore, USA 1981.

2. Holder M. & Wood R. — *Reality orientation.* Churchill-Livingstone, London & New York, 1982

3. Reisberg B. — *A guide to Alzheimer's disease for families, spouses and friends.* Free Press, New York, & Collier-MacMillan, London, 1981.

4. Powell L. & Courtice K. — *Alzheimer's disease, a guide for families.* Addison-Wesley, USA & UK, 1983.

5. Pearce J.M.S. — *Dementia; a clinical approach.* Blackwell Oxford, U.K., 1984.

6. Mayeux & Rosen (Editors) — Raven press series, Advances in neurology, no: 38. *The dementias.* Pub. RavenPress, New York, 1983.

7. Bright R. — *Practical planning in music therapy for the aged.* Alfred International, Sherman Oaks, CA, 1984

8. Bright R. — *Grieving.* MMB Music, Inc. St Louis, 1986.

9. Stephens M. — *You're never too old to learn.* A book of programmes for cognitive stimulation, including music. From B & S Books, 42 Caledonian Avenue, Winston Hills, NSW 2153, Australia.

AUTHOR INDEX

TOPIC INDEX

TOPIC INDEX